Rejoice!

GOSPEL MEDITATIONS

Rejoice!

GOSPEL MEDITATIONS

LOUIS EVELY

Translated by J. F. Bernard

DOUBLEDAY & COMPANY, INC.

GARDEN CITY, NEW YORK

1974

The material in this book consists of selections from *Meditations d'Evangiles*, published by Editions Universitaires (Paris, 1973).

Library of Congress Cataloging in Publication Data

Evely, Louis, 1910-
Rejoice! Gospel meditations.

Translation from Méditations d'Évangiles.
1. Bible. N.T. Gospels–Meditations. I. Title.
BS2555.4.E9413 1974 242
ISBN 0-385-05994-9
Library of Congress Catalog Card Number 74-6796

Printed in the United States of America
First Edition

CONTENTS

FOREWORD

These meditations are offered to provide the reader with material for meditation on the Gospels. The sole end of these meditations is to make the Gospel speak to contemporary man. In order to achieve that end, it is indispensable that the reader read the Gospel texts for himself. This book is intended to be a complement to the work of the Evangelists, and not a substitute for it.

It will be noted that the parallelism of the three Synoptic Gospels has often encouraged the author to clarify and supplement the meaning of one Evangelist by referring to the other two.

And finally, it will be obvious that these pages are not designed to be read in one sitting, but to be meditated bit by bit, day after day, according to the needs of the individual and to the time at his disposal.

Part One

SAINT MATTHEW

–1–

ON SUFFERING

Happy those who mourn . . . (Matthew 5:5)

Though the world mourns, no one comforts it. And there are many who weep and will never be consoled. Suffering and evil are a mystery that outrages our reason and tries our faith.

It is useless to try to explain suffering and evil by sin alone. Certainly, sin is responsible to a greater or lesser extent; but long before man sinned the world had been created in such a way as to include pain, the struggle for life, death, and dissolution, as its essential elements.

How could God have conceived and created such a world? And how can man explain the fact that God did so? We can always deny that God is the cause of evil—but that only makes the world seem even more absurd than it already is. What we must do, in effect, is to admit the existence of both ends of the chain of creation without seeing how the two ends are connected. That is, we must admit both the hideous reality of evil and the extraordinary presence of goodness and beauty.

Jesus did not explain the presence of evil in the world. Instead, he consoled us by revealing that God also suffers from evil. God also strives against evil. God also is mysteriously helpless in the face of evil. But God rises above evil and overcomes it by the all-encompassing strength of his love.

God's love is strong enough to bring consolation to us who suffer, not by waving a magic wand in order to change our tears into laughter but by teaching us to love as he loves, so that our love may drown our suffering.

It is unworthy of us to close our eyes when we see suffering in the world. We can call ourselves Christians only if we believe in a love stronger than death and stronger than evil.

We are happy only if we are incapable of buying happiness cheaply, at a discount. Happy the man who knows that the world is sick, that life is impossible, that man is perverted. Happy the man who knows, as Hamlet did, that there is something "rotten in the state of Denmark." The greatest suffering that we can have is not to know that we suffer; not to realize that to be human is to suffer.

Suffering is like a light. It can be harsh, and it can be unwelcome. It is not always something that makes us virtuous. But it *is* always something that reveals a truth to us.

A man who suffers is a man who has been informed and initiated. In the midst of a world of unknowing creatures, he is aware that he has not been made for that sinful world. He has been alerted that the world must be changed, converted —turned upside down. It is true that man's greatest enemy is his intellectual laziness, sustained unawareness, and perennial distraction; but it is equally true that death and suffering are the only inevitable factors of human existence that compel man to question, to reflect, to ask himself what life means and how it can be eternalized.

The burden of suffering, when we look at it face-on, is heavy indeed. No one can bear it without running the risk of being crushed. It is a characteristic of evil to scandalize—that is, to confront the man who resists it with an evil that is as intolerable, if not more intolerable, than the first. When adolescents first discover the ugliness of the world, or the weaknesses of their parents and teachers, their usual reaction is to hate that ugliness and weakness and, simultaneously, to create a disastrous situation that reveals their own rage and weakness, their inability to bear the weight of evil.

Only the one who created the world is strong enough to bear the sins of the world. Only the one who died on the cross is capable of bearing the weight of the cross. We must not flee the sight of suffering in others; but at the same time, we must not allow ourselves to be overwhelmed by trying to bear it alone. The solution is to take refuge at the feet of the Crucified and to listen to him say: "Do not lose courage. I have conquered evil. Within myself, there is love sufficient to justify all existence, to vanquish all despair, to purify all sin." These words are not easy to understand. We must repeat them to ourselves over and over again, we must hear ourselves say them many times, before we dare believe them.

We have a natural inclination to regard suffering as a punishment, as a sign of God's enmity for us, or at least of God's indifference toward us.

It is of the essence of faith for us to recognize the ubiquity and the strength of evil, its ugliness and its injustice, and yet, at the same time, to appeal from evil to a Redemption that compensates for evil, to rely on the loyalty and tenderness of the Father for "no one is forgotten in God's sight" (Luke

12:6), and to continue our struggle against the evil which repels us.

In order to confront the mystery of evil in the world, we have no need of explanations and arguments. What we need is to participate in the battle against evil, to take part in the struggle to free our brothers from evil, to have sufficient love to convert our enemies. The solution to the mystery of evil lies not in our philosophies, or even in our theologies, but in the actions of every one of us. Through our actions, we will discover that evil is weaker than we had thought; that each of us has within himself a love strong enough to conquer evil. And thus we will come to share the invincible hope experienced by Christ during his Passion and expressed in a promise made to all those who suffer and mourn: "Today you will be with me in Paradise!"

–2–

ON MAKING PEACE

Happy the peacemakers: they shall be called sons of God. (Matthew 5:9)

In some of the older translations of the New Testament, this particular Beatitude was rendered: "Blessed are the peaceful, for they shall be called the children of God." The word "peaceful," however, is ambiguous. It is certainly good to love peace; but it is even better to work actively for peace. The use of the word "peaceful," therefore, ran the risk of being taken in its widest and most selfish meaning, as counseling us to hold ourself aloof from conflict and from problems so as not to disturb our tranquility. Those who are peaceful, in the latter meaning of the term, are certainly not the children of a God who was made flesh and threw himself into the midst of a religious, social, and political storm in order to end up on the cross.

The truly peaceful man is the man who *makes* peace; and, in order to make peace, he must spend his life on the battlefield, standing between the combattants whom he works to reconcile. This is hardly a position which has anything to do with "peace" in the sense of repose or tranquility.

The peace referred to and preached by the Evangelist is that which upsets and destroys the false security of the world.

It is a sword that divides, that is capable of raising brother against brother and citizen against citizen. Christian peace destroys the "established disorder" and is realized only when justice is accomplished.

And this is why Christ came to bring both *peace* and *the sword.*

It is true that Jesus did not make use of violent means. He did not try to seize power. He did not undertake an organized action to transform institutions immediately. Yet, he preached, and accomplished, the most decisive revolution the world has ever known.

First and foremost, that revolution was religious in nature. It revealed to us that God is not a master who wishes to be served. He is the servant who gives us life, breath, and nourishment. God commands us to love—not to love him, but to love our fellow men with his own love. God does not command us to worship him in the Temple, but to adore him in spirit and in truth, by "spiritual sacrifices" in our everyday lives.

Jesus desacralized everything that was regarded as sacred in his time by naturally religious men: worship, sacrifice, fasting, the Temple, the priesthood, the Sabbath, and the Law. He taught that the only absolutely sacred thing on earth was man himself, the son and image of God. We will be judged, he told us, not by our religious practices, but by our social relationships (Matthew 25:7–21 and Luke 13:25–30).

He combined practice with his preaching. He violated the most sacred laws and traditions of Israel. He encouraged his followers to undertake the same kind of "civil disobedience." And he put himself in open opposition to the authorities.

It was indeed a religious revolution, but one with immediate political implications. The religious power that Jesus opposed was, at the same time, a political and judicial power. Yet, he claimed for himself the power to modify institutions. He made himself greater than Jonas, Solomon, and Abraham; greater even than Moses, the great legislator of Israel. He taught with authority—not like the scribes, but as a legitimate leader of the Jewish people.

From the political and social standpoint, what is most important about that religious revolution is its long-term consequences. We must recall that the different "powers" are, in reality, a single power. Civil authority is sacralized because it has been modeled after the divine and ecclesiastical governments supporting them. Therefore, by effecting a radical change in the idea that man had of God—by revealing to us a God who is a servant, poor, humble, gentle, crucified—Jesus changed radically the exercise of political, social, and judicial power in the world. By abolishing "religion" (the complex of man's obligations to God) in favor of charity (our obligations toward our fellow men who are the true Temple of God, the true presence of God among us), Jesus revolutionized human relationships, and even the very concept of humanity.

It will take centuries for us to realize in practice that the leader must be the servant; that the value of a man is measured by the quality of his human relationships; that money is the most tyrannical of masters, and that it must be made to serve us by making friends for us who will welcome us into the eternal tabernacle.

Jesus, then, was a revolutionary. Not because he organized and achieved a revolution, but because he transformed men's minds in such a way as to transform all of man's institutions.

Certainly, it is not necessary to be a Christian in order to be a revolutionary. But can a man really be a Christian in a world where his fellow men are starved, oppressed, degraded, and abandoned, without working for a revolution? That is, without becoming a peacemaker?

–3–

ON MERCY

Happy the merciful: they shall have mercy shown them. (Matthew 5:7)

In God forgiveness is joy. Nothing pleases God more than to exercise compassion. ". . . there will be more rejoicing in heaven over one repentant sinner than over ninety-nine virtuous men who have no need of repentance" (Luke 15:7).

Jesus found fault with the Pharisees, with the elder brother of the Prodigal Son, with the workers of the first hour, because they did not rejoice in the good fortune of their brothers—but especially because they did not share God's joy in opening his heart to grant free pardon.

One of the Fathers of the Church, in writing a line-by-line commentary on Genesis, reached the words: "God made man, and then rested." Why, the good Father wondered, did God need to rest after creating man? He had already created all the choirs of angels, and he did not rest. He had created the heavens and the earth and all that they contain, and there was no indication that he was tired. He had created the countless species of plants, and all the animals from the flea to the elephant, and nowhere did Genesis say that he had rested from this mighty labor. But "he made man, and then rested." Why? Finally, the commentator came up with the explanation. "Animals," he said, "cannot be forgiven, because they are not responsible for what they do. And angels cannot be forgiven, because, whatever they do, they cannot repent, since they are totally present in each one of their acts. But men and women are strange creatures. They never truly want to do what they do, and they never truly do what they want to do. Such creatures can be forgiven because they can repent. They can be consoled when they are sorry for having done something wrong. Therefore, if God rested after having created man, it was because he had finally found someone to whom he could act as God, to whom he could show himself as the Father—someone whom he could forgive."

Giving is easy for God. But forgiving, continuing to give to someone who gives nothing in return and who forgets to be grateful, showering gifts on someone who offends him, and especially welcoming with ineffable grace, warmth and tenderness, someone who returns to God after having betrayed him—this is the perfect gift, the quintessential gift which it is God's joy to give and which he longs to give.

Our God does not "give to each his due." He does not "reward the just and punish the wicked." Instead, he offers this paradox of love: "Love your enemies, do good to those who hate you, pray for those who treat you badly." And, unbelievable as it may seem to us, God himself does what he commands us to do. He loves his enemies. He lavishes his gifts on those who offend him. And, even on the cross, he prays for his executioners.

Mercy, therefore, is the characteristic sign of the Christian, not because it is so difficult as to be impossible to those who do not believe, but because it creates an essential resemblance between God and the Christian. God is merciful. God is the friend of sinners (Luke 7:34). God has compassion on the people; and, if he has favorites among the people, those favorites are the poor. Those who love their enemies, those who render good for evil, those who forgive those who persecute them—these are the ones who are like the Father. They are the sons of the Father "who makes the sun to rise on the wicked as on the good, who causes the rain to fall on the just and on the unjust." These are the men who are happy with God's happiness.

God's joy in forgiving has only one limitation, and that is the limitation imposed by a man whom he forgives but who refuses, in his turn, to forgive. God does not punish such refusal by withholding his mercy from the ungrateful sinner. Indeed, he continues to offer his own forgiveness. But, while waiting for the recipient of that forgiveness to exercise forgiveness on his own, God surely notes that nothing of himself has entered into the man, that the divine influence has not touched him. For if there is a decisive proof that God's pardon has been fruitless, sterile, and alien in a sinner, it is that the sinner refuses, in his turn, to grant pardon.

There are no arbitrary commandments or fabricated sanctions of our own happiness. God himself cannot make us happy if we stubbornly refuse to love. God cannot share his happiness with us if we are not willing to share his tastes, his character, his love, and his forgiveness. God's sole joy is to love boundlessly; and only those will taste that joy who abandon themselves to his divine and eternal folly.

-4-
ON PURITY

Happy the pure in heart: they shall see God. (Matthew 5:8)

The purity of heart to which Matthew refers is obviously not the legalistic purity of the Jews nor the sexual taboos of the Jansenists. A pure heart is a simple heart; a heart absorbed by God and the Kingdom; a heart open to the Word and willing to be pruned by it (John 15:3).

The impure heart is one that claims to serve God and Mammon simultaneously. When a man is concerned only with his own interests but pretends to seek only the interests of others, when he searches out a commendable motive for satisfying his vices while making a great display of virtue so as to enhance his standing in the eyes of the world, that man's heart is contaminated and impure.

There was nothing Jesus detested more than hyprocrites who preached but did not practice, who placed intolerable burdens on the shoulders of others while refusing to lift a finger themselves, and who, even in the presence of God himself, worried only about the impression they were making on others. The minds and hearts of these men are filled with such ambiguity and contradiction that they themselves do not know what they want. They have consecrated themselves to God. They recite prayers, perform rituals, undertake fasts, and distribute alms. But their true consolation lies in the notice that other men take of them.

The man who is pure in heart searches first of all for the Kingdom of God and his justice, and the rest is given to him automatically. He is not divided, torn, split between different ends, which, by reason of this inner conflict, he is unable to attain. What he does is rendered effective by the very simplicity of his intention. And, since he is concerned with no one but God, he enters into easy and happy communication with God. In a very real sense, such a man "sees God."

It has been said that a man cannot see God and continue to live. Certainly, a man cannot see God and continue to live in pride, greed, and distraction. A man cannot see God and continue to live as he did before knowing God. A man cannot see God and continue to follow any master whose teachings satisfy his whim of the moment. We cannot see through a dirty windowpane; and we cannot see God through a heart sullied by selfish preoccupations and cares.

Only a heart that is pure—that is, free—can see God, feel God, taste God. When we complain about the absence or silence of God, it can only be because our hearts are so encumbered by concerns other than God that we can neither see him nor hear him. The pure in heart see God because they are sensitive to the things that are most important to themselves. "Where your treasure is, there also is your heart"—and your eyes. Only the man who looks shall find. And only the man who knocks is promised a response. "The bridegroom knows the bride by a single hair from the nape of her neck," says the Song of Songs. Only the indifferent bridegroom asks to see his bride's identity card. By a thousand signs that pass unnoticed by others, the man who is pure in heart recognizes and welcomes the presence of God. He sees it in the strength he derives from prayer, in the peace he experiences when he has been faithful to the inspiration he has received, and in the remorse he feels when he has resisted that inspiration. He sees it when he has accepted a sacrifice with generosity, and when, after a particularly difficult struggle, he realizes that he has risen above himself through the strength of Another.

Like Mary, the man who is pure in heart stores up the experiences of his life in his heart and meditates over them in order to discover God in them. It often happens that he does not understand immediately; but he has had too much experience with God to be discouraged over this initial failure. He knows that he will eventually understand that which for the moment eludes him. He has already received enough light to be able to bear darkness for a while. He is certain that soon he will catch sight of his guide again.

The pure heart understands and loves the things of God. God is naturally visible to the man whose eyes have been purified. In Eden, Adam talked with God in the cool of the evening. And Moses spoke to God face to face, as a man does with a friend. For us, too, when we are humble, poor, and pure in heart, the Word is made flesh and lives among us and with us. If we do not see the Word, it is because we have not opened ourselves to him. The light shines today, as always, in the midst of darkness. Only men who are of darkness refuse to let it shine upon them.

The normal condition of humans is to see God in those around us and in the events of our lives. Even when Jesus walked among men, there were those among his contemporaries who saw him, touched him, heard him—and yet refused to acknowledge his presence. These same men complained of God's absence and pretended to long for a sign from heaven. They, like us, did not like the way in which God chose to reveal himself to us.

Only a few of Jesus' contemporaries—a few men who were pure in heart—felt themselves moved at his presence. Only a few felt themselves drawn to Jesus by some mysterious, unexplainable force. As Jesus spoke, their hearts burned within them; and those who were of God heard the word of God resound within themselves. The sheep know the voice of the shepherd and run to follow him. But when these few returned to their homes, astonished and changed by an extraordinary happiness, their friends and family asked: "What did he say? What did he do that was so wonderful? What proof did he give? What makes you believe in him?" And it was impossible to answer. Jesus' followers remained silent, so as to remember and to re-create the happiness that he had inspired in them. They could only say: "No man has ever spoken as this Man. Only God can forgive sins as this Man does. There has never been a greater love . . ."

God is no more and no less visible than love itself. When a man truly loves, his love is visible. Other men see it and know that the Spirit of God is present. In the early Church, only men "filled with the Spirit" were chosen for important missions. And the pagans said of the first Christians, "*See* how they love one another!" The love of these Christians was such that, through it, God himself was made visible. The pagans themselves could not help envying those who lived in the purity of heart that is devoted to a single love and preferred that love to the riches and joys of the world.

When there is love in a community or in a family—and also, unfortunately, where there is no love—it is visible to the whole world. Nothing could be clearer.

Let us not ask God for "signs." He has already given us love, which is sign enough. We have only to see it and cultivate it. Our only prayer should be one asking for the courage to radiate that love by removing all the obstacles with which we have surrounded it.

–5–

ON PERSECUTION

Happy those who are persecuted in the cause of right: theirs is the kingdom of heaven! (Matthew 5:10)

Jesus said it to the poor, and now he repeats it for those who are persecuted: the Kingdom of Heaven is theirs.

The persecuted are, in fact, a species of the poor. They are those who are poor because they have been despoiled and mistreated by others. The violence to which they have been subjected makes their poverty more difficult to bear and more repellant; but Jesus consoles them by unveiling the reality hidden under the appearances: they have entered into the Kingdom—albeit unwillingly. Even though they were subjected to violence, that violence was instrumental in ridding them of those things that might have distracted them from God or even wooed them away from him. They may have lost their worldly goods, or their good names; but they will never be stripped of that passion for justice for the sake of which they have suffered.

Persecution is the ineluctable fate of all those who hunger and thirst for justice. Such people do not conform. They protest, contest, and generally disturb the universally triumphant order of established injustice. Therefore, they are made to pay for their temerity. When a man works for justice—whether it is the justice of God or that of man—he always creates resentment. This resentment often reaches such a pitch that he becomes the victim of role-reversal, in the sense that he is accused of persecuting either those who were persecuting him or those whom he is trying to prevent from persecuting others.

The consolation of the man who is working for justice is the joy and gladness to which he has been invited by Jesus; that is, the knowledge that he is acting as one who has entered the Kingdom, who shares the work of God, who has the Prophets as his models and Jesus as his companion on the Cross. No one has endured greater persecution for justice's sake than God. God has gone before and inspired all those who later learn to recognize themselves in God, to accept their sufferings, and to rejoice in the fact that they have begun to resemble God.

The happiness of those who resemble God in this respect does not consist in some vague promise for the future, and much less in a hope of vengeance. Their happiness is the experience they have undergone, the impulse that led them to subject themselves to persecution for the sake of justice. That impulse is an inspiration from God, a communication of God's sentiments, an immediate sharing of God's happiness with man. And, for that reason, such men prefer to be the persecuted rather than the persecutors. They prefer to suffer injustice rather than to inflict it. And they know that this was precisely what they had in mind when they became Christians, for Jesus himself said it: "Anyone who does not take his cross and follow in my footsteps is not worthy of me. Anyone who finds his life will lose it; anyone who loses his life for my sake will find it" (Matthew 10:38–39).

What Jesus means is that the man who loses his life for Jesus' sake will find his real life. This man will realize—not only in the afterlife, but here and now on earth—that he lives not his own life but the life of God. He will know the great things that God has done for him in the midst of poverty and suffering. He will see that those who are persecuted in the cause of right are indeed happy.

The lot of the Christian is not, as some people think, to be sad and miserable. People who believe this have understood only one part of the Beatitudes—and the worst part, at that. They think that in order to obey Christ they must be poor, that they must weep and mourn, that they must seek out persecution. They tell themselves: All right, I'll deprive myself so as to give alms. I'll be sad. I'll go hungry. And, so far as persecution goes, I have an employer (or a wife, or husband, or a mother-in-law) who will be more than happy to oblige me in that respect.

Such platitudes are unworthy of the teaching of Christ. Jesus does not tell us to be sad, or poor, or hungry, or persecuted. What he does tell us is to be *happy*—happy when we are poor, happy when we are persecuted, happy even when we are miserable. It's too easy to be happy when one is rich; and too commonplace to be sad when one is poor. We are manifestations of God, witnesses to God, only when we are like him; that is, only when we find our happiness in poverty and gentleness, in a thirst for justice and a passion for persecution. It is only then that we prove we are living with a love that enables us to bear anything. It is only then that we know God has opened his Kingdom to us and poured out its treasures on us. It is only then that we can be certain God has taught us to love as he loves.

The most untenable interpretation of the Beatitudes is that which construes them as a promise for the hereafter, or as an assurance that in heaven things will be different. The silliest thing we can believe is that those who are poor on earth will be rich in heaven, or that those who are sad here below will be happy in the Kingdom. If that were the correct interpretation, then it would be wrong for us to try to feed the hungry or to console those who mourn, for in so doing we would be threatening their salvation. What we would have to do, in such a case, would be to reduce as many people as possible to poverty, to make the whole world miserable, so that everyone could be saved.

Jesus does not ask us to do the absurd. For him, the poor and the persecuted are happy here on earth, not because they are poor or persecuted, but because they know that the Kingdom is already theirs.

The rich man stores up great wealth, not a penny of which will he be able to take with him when he dies. The rich man is a lonely man because he must keep his fellows at a distance in order to protect his possessions. The rich man is a slave because he belongs to his possessions rather than being their master.

The poor man, on the other hand, is a member of a family. He has a Father who shares everything he has with his children and who teaches them to love and to give as he himself does. He has brothers with which he is in joyful communication. He wins friends by means of the "tainted money" of which Jesus spoke (Luke 16:9), and he rejoices in sharing that money rather than in keeping it all to himself. The poor man is the master rather than the slave of his possessions. He has wealth, and he makes use of it. He increases it, and he shares it. If there comes a time when he has no more wealth, then he has friends who are worth more than money in the bank.

In the final analysis, the poor man loses nothing even by death. Death does not change him, since he is, on earth, as he will be in heaven. He is eternally a son, eternally a brother, eternally a free man.

Happy the poor. Happy the persecuted. Happy the unhappy. For the Kingdom of God is theirs already!

–6–

ON BEING THE SALT OF THE EARTH

You are the salt of the earth . . . you are the light of the world. (Matthew 5:13–14)

When we hear Jesus tell us that we are the salt of the earth and the light of the world, it does not make us feel very proud of ourselves. To us modern Christians, his words sound like reproaches. It would be more in keeping with reality for us to recognize that we are useless servants rather than "the salt of the earth"; and that, if we are "the light of the world," we have kept that light pretty well hidden under bushel baskets.

Let us look at the facts. In the past few centuries, what exactly have we accomplished? How many wars have we stopped? (It would be far easier to count those we have started.) What injustices have we abolished? (There is a long list of those we have perpetrated.) Precisely what racial, social, cultural, national, or religious barriers have we destroyed so that all men might see that they are brothers?

There have been great revolutions in the past two hundred years; revolutions in scientific, social, and political thought. New philosophies have been devised, new sciences developed, new forms of government evolved. The world has gone from universal absolution to democracy and socialism. Universal tolerance has been proclaimed. Vast areas have been freed from domination by colonial powers. Women have been emancipated. And what exactly have we Catholics contributed to all this? In most cases, we contributed only our active opposition—despite the fact that all of these things form part of the Revelation of Christ.

Salt of the earth? Light of the world? Fortunately, Jesus did not intend these to be words of praise for what we have done. Instead, they are supposed to move us to examine our consciences and to see how far we have fallen short of our ideal. When Jesus says, "You are the salt of the earth, you are the light of the world," he is not congratulating us for what we have done. He is commanding us to place ourselves at the service of mankind.

We will become the salt of human love only when we learn to honor the joining together of human bodies sufficiently for us to realize that such union is neither a "mortal sin" nor a brief and meaningless pastime, but the expression of a mature, tested love.

We will become the light of the world only when we find a remedy to the terrible isolation of individuals by creating living, fraternal, joyful communities of humans—communities to which men will be drawn when they see how much their inhabitants love one another.

We will be what God wants us to be only when we set an example for a world increasingly divided into rich and poor, oppressors and oppressed, by voluntarily sharing our goods, our knowledge, and our power with those who are deprived of these things.

We will give meaning to human labor only when we allow workers a share in both management and profits.

We will give hope to a cynical and despairing world only when we are able to demonstrate what a small group of humans can accomplish by giving of themselves without regard to their own personal interests.

We must create houses of prayer, not as havens for those who want to flee from the world, but as centers of renewal and as training camps where we may learn to lead active lives without exhausting our resources, to refresh ourselves by means of our work, and to receive in accordance with what we give.

We must proclaim the Gospel for our time—the words of joy and freedom that the Lord can speak only in our own hearts and through our mouths.

In the light of such a program of action, we will begin to understand how much we are lacking, and what our Gospel for today signifies. If we give so little light, it is because we are not sufficiently transparent. We block the rays emanating from the only true light of the world because we are not sufficiently permeated with the strength, freshness, and vigor of his Word.

In order to attract the world to himself, Christ must present an image to mankind. And the only image at his disposal is our own; that of our fraternal Christian communities. It is easy to understand, therefore, why the world is not yet converted to Christ.

Nonetheless, Christ is in us as an inexhaustible source of light, strength, and self-renewal. We must be the first to turn to him, the first to realize what he came to announce. We should remember what kind of men the disciples were whom

Jesus called the salt of the earth and the light of the world. They were no stronger, no more intelligent, and no more courageous than we are. The difference is that they loved a Master who was able to make his inspiration evident in their words and his strength manifest in their weakness.

The message that the Christian must announce to the world is not a message of Christian virtue or Christian superiority. It has nothing to do with our personal qualities. Left to ourselves, there is nothing within us personally that can be communicated to the world. Only God can be communicated. Only God can live in us without making us cease to be ourselves. We can bear witness to the world only concerning that which God has accomplished in us; for what God has done in us, he can also do in others.

From that standpoint, it makes little difference that a man may be naturally strong, courageous, healthy, generous, and pure. But it does make a difference if a man was once weak, and God has strengthened him; if he was once impure, and God has purified him and made him happy; if he was once troubled, and is now at peace; if he was once timid, and is now confident; if he was once a miser, and is now openhanded; if he was once bent on vengeance, and has now learned to forgive. This is what matters in the world. Weakness, impurity, fear, greed, resentment—these are the things that the Christian has in common with the world; and, since the world believes in these things, it can also believe in the healing of them.

–7–

ON BEARING OUR TRIALS AND TRIBULATIONS

Do not be afraid . . . (Matthew 10:26–33)

"The most effective witness that we can bear to Our Lord," said Father de Foucauld, "is never to be afraid."

The fact is, fear is a sign that we lack faith. Jesus often reproached his Apostles for their fear—a fear that was based upon an accurate estimate of the apostles' abilities, but forgot to take into account the divine strength they shared. We, like they, have access to unlimited resources. Jesus himself has said it: "Everything you ask and pray for, believe that you have it already, and it will be yours" (Mark 11:24). Jesus did not tolerate fear in his followers even in the midst of a tempest, even when those followers were summoned to appear before the kings and princes of the world. And, after his followers had abandoned him, denied him, and betrayed him, the first thing Jesus said to them was: "Do not be afraid!"

When we are afraid, it is because we place our trust in ourselves rather than in God. And when we are fearless, it is because we have the audacity of our faith in God. We believe that nothing is impossible to God—or to us, in God.

Fearlessness is absolutely essential to an effective apostolate. If we are to bear witness before the world, as Jesus tells us to, we must have total faith in the presence and love of Jesus; for only the strength of our faith proves the reality of what we believe in, and only it makes the object of our faith present and visible to others.

At the same time, we must have a fairly exact idea of divine Providence and of what we can expect from it. Is it true, as the Evangelist assures us, that not a hair falls from our heads unless the Father wills it? Is it really God's will that we be subjected to pain and loss—not to mention baldness? It is frightening to think so; yet, many Christians are convinced that God wants us to suffer. "It is God's will!" they say piously, when a disaster is so overwhelming that it seems to surpass even the human capacity for evil. "God has taken your husband," we tell the widow; and bereaved parents are assured that "God has taken your child to himself."

Such sentiments bear the seeds of atheism, for who could believe in a God who would deprive a woman of her husband, or parents of their children? To believe that God is the author of evil is not only illogical, but it is also plainly at variance with the whole spirit of the Gospel. The Jesus of the Gospels does not kill, he raises from the dead; he does not afflict, but heals. He restores the son to his mother, the daughter to her father, the brother to his sisters. He does not separate. He unites. He neither judges nor punishes; instead, he warns sinners of what the future holds for them.

God is love; and love does not seek evil or work evil. Rather, love suffers evil from those who are loved.

Certain timid persons suggest that evil occurs "without God's permission." God, in other words, is a helpless spectator to human suffering—if he does not actually contribute to it by a sort of tacit acquiescence.

It is impossible to believe that God either works evil or is helpless in the face of evil. And far from allowing evil, God is opposed to it. He could not bear to see us suffer and die, and so he came down among us to suffer and die himself so that we might be delivered from evil through the revelation of a love strong enough to overcome all evil. For this reason, God recognizes himself in those who thirst and hunger after justice, and in those who struggle against evil. He does not recognize himself in those who "permit" evil so as to maintain a prudent neutrality. God himself is against all evil; and he is the inspiration of everyone who fights against evil.

Yet, God is love, and he does not exercise a capricious or despotic power over evil. He opposes evil by loving and by communicating that love to us so that we, too, may oppose evil and deliver the world from it. The compassionate God who chose to die on the cross is not the whimsical Jupiter of the pagans, wielding the thunderbolt to punish his enemies. It is by being raised up on the cross that God wishes to draw mankind to himself—not by descending from the cross in a divine fury to terrify and punish those who have offended him. Force, authority, and prestige are all rendered powerless by the cross. Only love retains its power. For it is from the cross that Jesus loves, converts, and pardons.

The Gospel does not say that when a hair falls from our heads it does so with the permission of the Father or because the Father allows it. The implication is clear that when we lose a hair it is not upon the initiative of the Father. But it is equally clear that when we lose our hair it is with the knowledge of the Father. The Father notices the loss. He gives us the grace to accept this loss; to rise above it in such a way that, incredible as it may seem, we may be happier bald than we were with hair!

The true meaning of Providence is that God is neither responsible for the evils we suffer, nor is he a shield against the threat of evil. God does not send disaster upon us, nor does he protect us against disaster. Instead, he is with us when we suffer disaster. He inspires us to love, to struggle, and to hope in the midst of disaster.

In his Epistle to the Romans, Saint Paul tells us precisely what to expect from God: "Nothing therefore can come between us and the love of Christ, even if we are troubled or worried, or being persecuted, or lacking food or clothes, or being threatened or even attacked. As scripture promised, 'For your sake we are being massacred daily, and reckoned as sheep for the slaughter.' These are the trials through which we triumph, by the power of him who loved us. For I am certain of this: neither death nor life, no angel, no prince, nothing that exists, nothing still to come, not any power, or height or depth, nor any created thing, can ever come between us and the love of God made visible in Christ Jesus our Lord" (8:35–39).

–8–

ON TRUE DETACHMENT

> *The kingdom of heaven is like treasure hidden in a field . . . the kingdom of heaven is like a merchant looking for fine pearls . . . the kingdom of heaven is like a dragnet cast into the sea . . .* (Matthew 13:44–52)

The three parables that conclude the thirteenth chapter of Matthew are hardly to be taken literally. Jesus tells us that "The kingdom of heaven is like treasure hidden in a field, which someone has found; he hides it again, goes off happy, sells everything he owns and buys the field." Obviously, he does not mean to imply that the actions of the man in the parable are commendable or appropriate as a model for our own. The sense of the parable, however, is quite clear. Jesus is advising us to find a value that will free us from everything we now think important; a treasure that will allow us to be numbered among the happy poor; an attachment that will allow us to detach ourselves from all else.

Traditional Christian education encouraged detachment in an exclusive sense. We were supposed to be detached from possessions and from persons, even from life and from happiness. Christianity was thus characterized by sacrifice and by a preoccupation with suffering. We insisted so much on the obligation to renounce everything that we forgot to mention the obligation to discover what justified this renunciation.

Yet, Christianity essentially is not a renunciation but an exercise in preference. The man who sells all his goods to buy the field containing buried treasure, the merchant who sells everything to buy an extraordinary pearl—these men are not masochists. Nor are they ascetics. They are astute individuals who recognize a good investment when they see it.

Jesus never told us to "mortify" ourselves. The term "mortification," once so common in Catholic schools, came to lose its true meaning. To mortify means to kill, to put to death. Saint Paul advised us to mortify our bad habits because they deformed us, preyed upon us, and eventually destroyed us. He told us to mortify our selfishness, our envy, our pride—but only so that we could live at our full potential.

When a Christian renounces something, it should be only for him to be able to acquire something better, for him to know greater happiness beginning "now, in the present time" (Mark 10:30). The Christian does not go out looking for the cross any more than a good worker goes out looking for an on-the-job accident. Yet, the Christian, like the worker, knows that accidents are an occupational hazard. He accepts the risk in order to do what he is supposed to do; that is, in the case of the Christian, to remain faithful to God and to his brothers. Jesus himself did not go out of his way to suffer. He loved mankind, and mankind compelled him to suffer; so, Jesus preferred love and suffering to non-suffering and non-love.

When we accept the cross, it should be only so that we may learn a higher love. We must "mortify" ourselves only so that we may rise from the dead stronger than ever. A seed dies in order to increase and grow—except that it does not really die. Instead, it acquires a superabundance of life and fruitfulness.

There is one death that the Christian is absolutely forbidden to seek, and that is a death which is sterile. Death for the sake of death. "Embrace the cross!" we used to say. "Seek out humiliation! Die to human nature!" The other kind of death, however, is that which consists of loyalty, faith, the giving of self, and love. This is the death that expands and multiplies life a hundredfold. "I am the true vine," Jesus tells us, "and my father is the vinedresser. Every branch in me that bears no fruit he cuts away, and every branch that does bear fruit he prunes to make it bear even more" (John 15:1–2).

It has been said too often that the death of Christ on the cross was "a failure, humanly speaking." The truth is that it was a magnificent triumph of human loyalty and love. Jesus, the man, accomplished his mission despite the fact that he was abandoned, betrayed, and tortured. He kept the faith until the end. He loved even when he knew "that the hour had come for him to pass from this world" (John 13:1). And his love made his death give birth to life immediately in the conversion of the thief, of the centurion, and of those who "went home beating their breasts" (Luke 23:48). Already Christ had risen from the dead. It was not the resurrection of three days later that turned the death of Christ into a great victory. It was the resurrection represented by his death itself; for such a death inspires the world more than any triumph possibly could. The Apostles themselves finally understood this. "You killed him, but God raised him to life, freeing him from the pangs of Hades; for it was impossible for him to be held in its power . . ." (Acts 2:24–25). They knew that another "spirit" was within them, and that with that Spirit they had crossed the threshold beyond which death held no terror for them. Christ had risen as a "mystical body" in the form of all those who had begun to live in him.

The essential thing for us Christians, therefore, is to find the one thing that makes it possible for us to give up everything else. It is fine for a man who has found a field containing a treasure to go out and sell everything he has in order to buy the field. But it would be foolish to give up everything that he has until he finds something better to take its place. If a man finds a matchless pearl, he has no need of lesser gems; but until he finds that one pearl of surpassing value, he would be well advised to hold on to the pearls that he has.

Anyone over thirty who has had a Catholic education can remember how often we were encouraged to undertake a course of negative conduct. "Renounce the world," we were told. "Give up the world in order to embrace the cross of Christ." And if a boy or girl decided to enter the religious life, they were solemnly advised that they had "chosen the difficult and painful path of mortification and sacrifice."

It seemed to occur to no one that one could have said the very same thing about marriage as about the religious life. In marriage, a man and a woman discover each other to the exclusion of all other men and women. Yet, no one emphasized the purely negative aspects of marriage. It never occurred to anyone to tell the groom: "Congratulations! You are giving up all the women in the world except your wife! What a marvelous example of sacrifice!" And I wonder what the reaction would have been if someone had told the bride: "My dear, this is the moment of your supreme sacrifice!

Woman is made to be a victim. You have chosen your cross, for you have taken it upon yourself to live with this one man for the rest of your days. And yet, you could have done better. After all, you are not bad looking. You had a good job. And, God knows, you had other proposals . . ."

When a man finds a treasure in a field, there is really no reason to congratulate him on his spirit of self-mortification or for having renounced the world. He is not being virtuous when he goes out and sells all that he has to buy the field. He is simply being logical and reasonable.

Yet, it does not often happen that men are logical and reasonable. Man is a strange being. He is capable of the most terrible sacrifice based upon a yearning for suffering or for self-destruction. But show him something that is obviously and incontestably good, and he quickly allows himself to be distracted by things that he knows are unimportant.

We must force ourselves to choose the precious treasure, the pearl of great price, over lesser goods. If we do not, we will find, on the last day, that we have lost not only the treasure and the pearl but also all that we kept in place of the treasure and the pearl.

–9–

ON FORGIVENESS

. . . *And so the kingdom of heaven may be compared to a king who decided to settle his accounts with his servants* . . . (Matthew 18:21–35)

Human society survives only because there is such a thing as forgiveness. Daily life inevitably engenders conflicts and differences which, just as inevitably, must be forgiven. There are, of course, communities where there is no forgiveness; and existence in such places constitutes a suitable foretaste of hell. But anyone who has experienced forgiveness knows that a plausible explanation can settle almost any difference, and that the joy of reconciliation is even greater than that of mutual understanding.

The Apostles, as a group, were frequently torn by envy, intrigue, and arguments. Time and time again, Jesus urged them to live in harmony with one another, to forgive one another, to be reconciled with one another. But, apparently, the words were no sooner out of Jesus' mouth than the Apostles were at it again, arguing among themselves over which of them would be the greatest man in the Kingdom.

Peter, an impetuous and somewhat belligerent man, was as quick to let his ambitions involve him in an argument as he was to repent when Jesus remonstrated with him. Once, perhaps in exasperation, he asked Jesus: "Lord, how often must I forgive my brother if he wrongs me? As often as seven times?"

Peter believed that he was being very generous in offering to forgive his brother seven times. Doubtless, he hoped to be able simultaneously to put his conscience at rest and to indulge his natural aggressiveness. But Jesus would have none of it. "Not seven," he answered, "but seventy-seven times" (Matthew 18:22).

It is safe to assume that Peter was somewhat discouraged at Jesus' response. "Seventy-seven times" obviously meant that Peter was wasting his time counting the number of times he would have to forgive. He was doomed to spend his whole life forgiving.

Jesus took advantage of the opportunity offered by Peter's question to recount the parable of the unforgiving debtor. A king, wishing to settle accounts with his debtors, called each one in and demanded his money. The first man could not pay, so the king had him and his family sold into slavery. The second man could not pay either, but threw himself down at the king's feet and asked for mercy. So, the king forgave him and canceled the debt. But then this same man, as he was leaving the king's presence, encountered someone who owed him money—and had his own debtor thrown into prison because he could not pay. The king, when he heard of this, had the merciless man "handed over to the torturers till he should pay all his debt."

The meaning of the parable is clear. God is the king and master who has loaned us more than we ourselves could ever afford to lend to anyone else: life, our senses, our bodies, nature, the heavens, the sea, the trees, the flowers. With respect to God, we are wasteful stewards, ungrateful servants, and insolvent debtors.

Luckily for us, our Master is more tender-hearted than we are. Like the king in the parable, God not only abstains from punishing us as soon as we ask for mercy, but he goes one step further: he forgives the entire debt. This is God's way. God is a Father, and his greatest joy is to give and forgive.

But what happens when a man's debt is forgiven by the Master, and that man has one of his own debtors imprisoned for a comparatively small debt? Certainly, if we were witnesses to such a scene we would be indignant at the unfairness of it all. Yet, we often do precisely what the ungrateful debtor did. God forgives us totally for terrible sins, and we in turn refuse to forgive those who have committed some slight offense against us, or we forgive them grudgingly or conditionally.

The concluding words of Jesus' parable are perhaps the most difficult to understand. "In his anger," Matthew records, "the master handed him over to the torturers till he should pay all his debt. And that is how my heavenly Father will deal with you unless you each forgive your brother from your heart." Surely, it would be wrong to believe that God is capable of anger; that he punishes, takes vengeance, or withdraws his forgiveness. God punishes no one. Men punish themselves by cutting themselves off from his blessings. God does not grow angry with us, or cause us harm. He loves us. And he loves us even when we sin, even when we persist in our sins, and even when we refuse to forgive although we ourselves have been forgiven.

It is true that the Gospels often speak of judgments and condemnations and punishments. What such terms signify, however, is not that God himself judges, condemns, and punishes the sinner, but that the sinner is judged, condemned, and punished—by himself. When the Master orders the unforgiving debtor to be "handed over to the torturers," does this mean that God will deprive the sinner of what he has and impose sanctions for his sins? Or does it mean simply that God takes cognizance of the state of the sinner?

If we believe that God is Love, we cannot also believe that God makes sinners suffer even more than they already suffer, or that he increases the unhappiness of those who are not happy. The divine light does not make the sinner miserable. It only shows how miserable the sinner is.

Even in the case of the unforgiving debtor, God loves the ungrateful man and is ready to forgive him once more for his terrible hardness of heart. But it is impossible for God to forgive a man who refuses to open himself to forgiveness by forgiving others. In such a case, God's pardon does not enter into a man. It does not "take" in the man who is impervious to pity. Even God cannot force a man to love. And when a man refuses to forgive, it is because he himself is not open to forgiveness.

When God sees that, despite the number of times he has forgiven us, we ourselves have not learned to forgive; when he sees that, notwithstanding his love for us, we have not learned to love, he does not withdraw his love and his forgiveness. But he does recognize that his own example of total forgiveness has not won us over, and that we have remained deaf to what he has so often tried to communicate to us.

The sense of the parable of the unforgiving debtor, therefore, is not that God condemns and punishes, but that he mercifully advises us of the consequences of our choice. In other words, when we refuse to forgive, God does not turn that refusal into a disaster for us. God simply lets us know that our refusal will end in disaster. He warns us of how terrible it is to live and die without hope and without love. He does not make it terrible. He merely tells us that it *is* terrible.

It is no exaggeration to say that if men imitated God's mercy, there would be no hell. For hell is a place where there is no forgiveness. Forgive, and you will be forgiven.

–10–

ON GOD'S GENEROSITY

The last will be first, and the first, last. (Matthew 20:16)

The parable of the vineyard laborers which opens the twentieth chapter of Saint Matthew is one of those rare passages from the Gospels capable of rousing a contemporary congregation to indignation. Good Christians are shocked to read that their Master's behavior apparently did not reflect the principles of justice and equity as they understand them.

We must remember that justice, essentially, consists in giving to each man that which is his due. Therefore, when the landowner in the parable decides to pay the latecomers the same amount as those who had been working in the vineyard all day, he is not being unjust. His unexpected generosity deprived no one of that which was rightfully his. At the same time, we must admit that the sentence with which Matthew ends the parable is somewhat misleading. "The last will be first," he says, "and the first, last." The fact is that the last are not first (except perhaps in the sense that they are paid first), and the first are not last. The owner of the vineyard treats everyone equally so far as pay is concerned.

What shocks us today is that the landowner gave equal pay for unequal work. We know that justice and equality are not the same thing. If we give everyone the same thing, then we end up giving too much to some and too little to others. In the parable, the owner of the vineyard is not concerned with justice but with generosity. From that perspective, it is to be expected that God is generous to everyone, and not only to the "last."

There is a weak point in the parable only if we interpret it as a complete and detailed description of the way things are done in the Kingdom. The fact is, however, that in the Kingdom everyone is rewarded out of all proportion to his merits and far beyond his wildest imaginings; for, what everyone receives from God is God himself.

In the parable of the vineyard laborers, Jesus wants to reproach those who complain because he is generous toward sinners. He tells them that they are wrong not to rejoice with him when those who were lost are found again. And he blames them especially for not sharing the divine happiness when God exercises his fundamental prerogative, which is to dispense mercy.

How often Jesus was reviled by the "just men" of his time, by those who received God's gifts as their due. It is no wonder that he preferred to be surrounded by publicans and sinners, by the humble, and by unbelievers—that is, by those who were capable of astonishment at God's generosity.

The Kingdom is no man's "due." It is a gift. We are in a position to receive that gift not because of our merits, or because we demand it, but because we open ourselves to God and acknowledge our own inadequacies. God is like a spring, but man must thirst before he can drink. God loves all men. He wants to shower his gifts on all men. Only one thing can prevent him from exercising his generosity: man himself, by refusing those gifts, or by being envious of the gifts of others, or by rationalizing God's gifts.

We must learn to receive the Kingdom as children receiving presents. That is, we must be like those who are not concerned with what is owed them, but who recognize that they have nothing except that which is given to them out of God's bounty and who receive with a joy proportionate to the Father's joy in giving.

-11-

THE WICKED HUSBANDMEN

There was a man, a landowner, who planted a vineyard; he fenced it around, dug a winepress in it and built a tower; then he leased it to tenants and went abroad. (Matthew 21:33-34)

When we hear or read the parable of the wicked husbandmen we recall the words ascribed to Jesus by Saint John: "I am the true vine" (15:1). Those who heard Jesus relate the parable, however, no doubt recalled the chant of Isaiah (5:1-2):

My friend had a vineyard
on a fertile hillside.
He dug the soil, cleared it of stones,
and planted choice vines in it.
In the middle he built a tower,
he dug a press there too.
He expected it to yield grapes,
but sour grapes were all that it gave.

The spirit of Jesus' parable is not very different from that of Isaiah. When the vintage time came around, Jesus explains, the landowner sent servants to collect his share of the produce; but the tenants mistreated the servants, killing one of them. Three times this happened. Finally, the landowner sent his son, saying, "Surely they will respect my son." Instead, the tenants killed the boy so that they might take over his inheritance.

At this point in the story, Jesus asked the chief priests and elders of the people what they thought the landowner would do to his wicked tenants. "He will bring those wretches to a wretched end," they replied, "and lease the vineyard to other tenants who will deliver the produce to him when the season arrives."

Jesus answered: "Have you never read in the scriptures:

> 'It was the stone rejected by the builders
> that became the keystone.
> This was the Lord's doing,
> and it is wonderful to see'?

I tell you, then, that the kingdom of God will be taken from you and given to a people who will produce its fruit."

God's plans are pursued in human history. But these plans are not precise designs that he accomplishes despite man's oppositions. Rather, they are forces that rise from the heart, they are a proposal of joy and peace addressed to man despite his sins and his lack of faith. God seeks to bring about an alliance between himself and a people upon whom he lavishes his goodness and generosity; a people in whom his gifts will bear fruit worthy of the giver. That is, a people who will love one another as God loves them. Thus, love, justice, and mercy will gradually permeate the world, and one day God's presence will be made visible and manifest in a world reconciled in his name. On that day, the Kingdom of God will be among us.

For centuries Israel believed that it would be the seed of

that Kingdom. The Israelites knew that they were the chosen people. They knew that they had been prepared for the Kingdom by the Law, readied for it by the Prophets. They viewed their selection as irreversible, as a hereditary privilege; and they made of it a matter of proud superiority over other peoples.

John the Baptist shocked them by preaching that God could turn the very stones of the desert into sons of Abraham; and Jesus shook them anew by announcing that the vineyard would be taken away from them and given to new tenants.

Until then, the Israelites had believed that they were the vineyard. Now, Jesus told them that they were only the tenants of the vineyard; that the true vineyard was the Kingdom, and that the Kingdom was present in Jesus—the same Jesus whom they would put to death without knowing what they were doing.

In the parable of the wicked husbandmen, Jesus appears as the new tenant, the tenant who will achieve and complete the history of Israel. After him, there would be no more Prophets sent by God, and the Kingdom would become the property of others.

But whose property has the Kingdom become? That of the Gentiles? Of the Church? Not necessarily. We should be very careful not to fall into the same way of thinking as the ancient Israelites and believe ourselves to be the proprietors of the Covenant, the incontestable heirs of the Kingdom. The only people whom Jesus recognized as his own are those "who will deliver the produce to him."

In other words, we Christians are in the same position as the chief priests and the elders whose questions Jesus answered in this parable, and who were as indignant as we are at the idea that we might not be, after all, the heirs of the Kingdom. Only a few lines earlier in the same chapter of Matthew, Jesus blamed the priests and elders for not believing John the Baptist though the truth of what he said was obvious even to "the tax collectors and prostitutes" (21:28–32). Do we treat our prophets any better than the Israelites did John the Baptist? We are quick to canonize saints after their death—just as quick as we were to persecute them when they were alive. It is certainly conceivable that the Second Coming of Jesus will find us no more faithful, vigilant, or watchful than Israel was at his first coming.

The essence of the parable of the wicked husbandmen consists not in a condemnation of others, but in an examination of our own consciences. Jesus announces his forthcoming death, not to complain or to bemoan his fate, but solely in order to warn his listeners of the terrible consequences of their hardness of heart. Are we really sure that our own hearts are not as hard as theirs, and that history is not about to repeat itself?

–12–

THE LAST JUDGMENT

When the son of man comes in his glory, escorted by all the angels, then he will take his seat on a throne of glory . . . (Matthew 25:31–46)

All of the events which we believe belong to the future, or which we very conveniently think will not happen in our lifetimes, are, in fact, present here and now. Eternal life has already begun. The "old things" are passing away. The Kingdom is now in our midst. Human beings are rising from the dead and being transfigured. Heaven and hell are already here on earth, in the hearts of men. And Judgment has already taken place (John 3:18). There is no need for God to judge us, for we have passed judgment on ourselves in our day-to-day lives. God will not even have to punish us or reward us, for each of us will go where we have made a place for ourselves—to that place where we have our roots and our treasure. Our relationships with our fellow men will determine forever our relationship with God.

Matthew presents this terrible revelation within the majestic framework of classical religion, in a spiritual, idealistic, and liturgical context. We are transported to the heavens, surrounded by angels. We stand before a throne wrapped in divine glory. Then, in order to emphasize brutal realism of judgment, the mighty King of Matthew's narrative says: "I was hungry. I was naked. I was in prison . . ." Now, we are suddenly brought back to earth. We are removed from the celestial realm to the Incarnation. The astonishment of mankind is total and universal. Both the good and the bad protest: "Lord, when did we see you hungry . . . or thirsty?"

There is something shocking here. Or rather, there is an element which is real, true, but paradoxical: the Incarnation is so troublesome, so inconvenient, that everyone seems to have forgotten it. We may well wonder whether, when the Son of Man returns he will find any faith at all left in the world. For those who believe in God have no faith in man; and those who have faith in man have turned away from God.

There is really no reason for us to be surprised. Jesus gave us fair warning that we would not be judged according to our religious practices. No one will ask us how many times we have prayed, "Lord, Lord . . ." No one will care what we have said or written, or how often we have made prophecies, chased out demons, or performed miracles. It will be irrelevant how much time we have spent listening to sermons, or attending "days of recollection" and retreats, or "laboratories" and "workshops." All of these exterior signs of intimacy with Jesus will count as nothing when the question arises of whether we should be grouped with the good or the bad on the day of Judgment. They will not be able to keep us from being thrown out of the Kingdom: "Go away from me, with your curse upon you, to the eternal fire prepared for the devil and his angels."

Here, it seems, it is revealed that we will not be judged according to our faith in God or in Jesus. Face to face with the

Lord, the just maintain that they did not recognize him in the people whom they served. But they were saved, nonetheless, because true faith in mankind and true love of mankind include implicitly faith and love in the God-Man, in the Word Incarnate, in Christ present in "the least of these." Christ did not accuse Saul of persecuting his followers. "I am Jesus," he declared, "and you are persecuting *me.*" It holds equally true to say: "I am Jesus, and you are serving *me.*" And, in fact, that is what the King says in Matthew's description of the Last Judgment. Therefore, it is less important for us to recognize and know God than it is for us to recognize and know our fellow man.

This passage of the Gospel contains some surprises for the formalistic Christian as well as for others. Salvation, we learn, is always a matter of personal discovery. We will be saved neither by obeying certain laws, nor by pious habits, nor by faithfulness to tradition. Here, as in the parables of the wise and foolish virgins, of the talents and of the treasure found in a field, there must be a certain element of surprise on our part—a finding, an act of personal initiative. Every man must act according to his own lights rather than by a set of rules imposed by others. He must take chances, without benefit of instructions or revelations that would relieve him of his personal responsibility for what he does.

Even religious instruction, it seems, plays little part in what we are. For everyone, believers and disbelievers alike, must wait till the Last Judgment to discover that God was made man, that the Word was their next-door neighbor, and that, in effect, the greatest commandment was really the commandment to love our neighbor.

The logical and essential question that arises from this passage on the Last Judgment is the following: Is it sufficient to love and serve our fellow men for us to be Christians? If so, what is the difference between a Christian and an honest, generous pagan? Can Christian revelation be summed up in one word: altruism? Is political activism really the up-to-date name for charity?

The word "love" has as many meanings as the name "God," and the manifestations of love must be studied as attentively and as critically as our religious practices. There are certain forms of love that are every bit as dangerous and destructive as indifference or outright oppression. We can make use of social activism as an excuse for not seeking out our own personal truth, or for ignoring the emptiness of our own lives. It often happens that we need other people only so that they may have need of us. We serve others, not so much because others need us, but because we need a way to lighten the burden of our own existence. There are "commitments" that are nothing more than an abdication of our critical sense and our personal responsibilities. There are battles against alienation that are themselves forms of alienation. And there are forms of militancy that rival religion as "the opium of the people."

For love to be authentic, it must be inspired, consciously or unconsciously. It must originate at a level at which it is given as freely as it is received.

The only "real life"—that is, the only life that is liveable eternally—consists in a kind of love that makes us rejoice in the happiness of others. It gives all and demands nothing. It nourishes us in proportion to the generosity with which we lavish it. It is a presence so convincing and absolute that, for its sake, we are equally willing to live forever or to die immediately.

This is the love that Jesus described as a conversion, as a new birth, as a life that will never end. If we are followers of Jesus, we know that his action within us is manifested only by means of that interior dimension: "The Son can do nothing by himself; he can do only what he sees the Father doing; and whatever the Father does the Son does too" (John 5:19). We know the importance of that perpetual and intimate communication which is love. "I am not alone," Jesus said, "the one who sent me is with me" (John 8:16).

The human life lived by Jesus was one in which a full relationship with God created a full relationship with man; one in which God, far from causing us to turn away from mankind and from the world, revealed the existence of our brotherhood with those who seem least like ourselves: with the poor, the humble, the prisoner, the ignorant, the sinner.

To be a Christian means to do as Christ did; that is, to take our inspiration from One who is greater than we and to give all that we have to our fellow men. There is only one Christian faith, and that faith consists in the continuous experience—a verified, controlled, critical experience—of the fact that it is not we who live, but Jesus who lives in us.

The Christian is not the man who is more virtuous, more capable, or more generous than another. He is simply a man who knows that he is *inhabited.*

these [illegible] made willing [illegible] to [illegible] an [illegible]

[illegible] used [illegible] record that [illegible] [illegible] followers of Jesus [illegible] that [illegible] him [illegible] [illegible] of [illegible] he himself [illegible] what [illegible] and when on [illegible] other [illegible] the Sabbath [illegible] we know [illegible] what [illegible] which [illegible]

[illegible] life [illegible] one of [illegible] [illegible] full [illegible] [illegible] and from [illegible] the [illegible] [illegible] the [illegible]

[illegible] Christian [illegible] [illegible] who [illegible] [illegible] and [illegible] [illegible] for [illegible]

[illegible] man who [illegible] [illegible]

Part Two

SAINT MARK

–13–

JESUS, THE PHARISEES, AND US

I did not come to call the virtuous, but sinners. (Mark 2:16–17)

If we base ourselves solely upon the Gospels, we must conclude that the Pharisees were a thoroughly contemptible group of people. According to the Evangelists, they were Jesus' bitterest enemies, and the character ascribed to them is wholly antipathetic. They are hardhearted men, devoid of sympathy for the poor and the humble. They carry formalism to the point of hypocrisy.

Yet, if we study the history and doctrines of the Pharisees objectively, we come up with a completely different estimate of them. They were men of commendable religious zeal and of courageous loyalty to their God and their Law. Normally, it would seem that they should have been Jesus' staunchest supporters. After all, it was the Pharisees who kept alive the Messianic expectations of the Jews and who were at the heart of Jewish religious practices. So far as their beliefs go, they were a progressive and spiritual group who, unlike the Sadducees, believed in the resurrection, in angels, and in spirits. The character of Gamaliel the Pharisee, as described in the Acts of the Apostles (5:34–39), for example, is a far cry from that of the Pharisees as depicted by the Evangelists.

In the light of such discrepancies, it is tempting to believe that perhaps the Evangelists have given us a distorted version of Jesus' attitude toward the Pharisees. Certainly, that attitude, as described in the Gospels, is totally lacking in mercy. Jesus nails the Pharisees to the wall at every opportunity. And there is not the slightest hint of any attempt to seek them out and to draw them to himself by friendly persuasion.

Even if we admit, for the sake of argument, that the Pharisees were as wicked and contemptible as the Evangelists claim they were, then it seems reasonable to believe that Jesus' love of sinners would have made him treat them with special consideration. If, as Luke tells (19:10) "The Son of Man has come to seek out and save what was lost," who was more in need of being sought out and saved than the Pharisees? After all, they were so lost that they finally crucified the Savior. Or are we to conclude that there are indeed sins so great as to discourage or ward off God's mercy?

We can conclude no such thing. At the same time, we must not believe that sin and sinners exercise an attraction for God. God is not drawn toward the greatest sin, nor even toward the greatest sinner. God is drawn to all men; but, among men, only those who have experienced their own weakness are open to God's forgiveness.

The sin of weakness makes man "grace-absorbent," as Charles Péguy puts it,* while sin makes us so impermeable to grace that all of God's mercy strives in vain against our own self-satisfaction.

* Péguy's phrase is: *mouiller à la grâce* (to be dampened by grace).

In the Gospel narrative, it is a source of inexhaustible astonishment to see humble sinners closer to Jesus than the virtuous Pharisees. The guilt of the sinner seems more fruitful than the morality of the just man. The key to the paradox, of course, is that Christianity is compatible with sin and weakness so long as sin and weakness are admitted, regretted, and struggled against. But it is not compatible with pride, even when that pride is based upon real values and upon efforts crowned with success.

A refusal to accept is more evil than a refusal to give. A man who accepts can receive the gift of being able to give; but a man who gives in pride simultaneously takes back, or turns back toward himself, and therefore sterilizes that which was capable of freeing him and causing him to open himself.

What emerges from the Gospel portrait of the Pharisees is precisely that. The Pharisees were proud of their faith, their knowledge, their good works, and their religious observances. Therefore, they were closed to God's gifts and to God's forgiveness, for they did not believe that they were in need of either. They regarded themselves as God's creditors. They were so filled with pride at having given and at having refused to accept, that they became incapable of either giving or forgiving.

Jesus' great reproach to the Pharisees was that they rejected God's mercy for themselves and refused to exercise mercy toward others. The eldest son, the Pharisee in the Temple, the workers of the first hour—all these figures from the Gospels and Jesus' parables had this in common: They all claimed they had certain rights. They all condemned sinners and were outraged at God's goodness. By their own merits, they were separated from God and made incapable of sharing God's pleasure in the forgiveness of sinners. They were no longer able to share in the joy of Christ or to feel wonder at the freedom and gratuitous nature of God's generosity. "I bless you, Father," Jesus said, ". . . for hiding these things from the learned and the clever and revealing them to mere children" (Matthew 11:25).

It is one of the paradoxes of human nature that we often find more generosity, compassion, and willingness to serve among libertines and loose women than among our moral rigorists. Now, as in the time of the Evangelists, the publicans and prostitutes precede the "just" and the pious into the Kingdom of Heaven. How strange it is that as soon as we come to believe that we possess truth and virtue, our hearts harden toward our fellow men! This, precisely, was what was wrong with the Pharisees. For, despite their undeniable virtues, they lacked that consciousness of their own inadequacy which would have opened them to God and to their fellow men.

The truth is that, for a Christian, there is no such thing as the *status quo*. We cannot be content with being a sinner; and we certainly cannot be satisfied with our virtues. We must always aim at perfection while, at the same time, acknowledging that we are the most miserable of sinners.

The danger implicit under the Old Covenant was that a man was capable of obeying the Law in its entirety. One could get by simply by obeying the Commandments—as did the rich young man who asked Jesus what he must do to possess eternal life (Matthew 19:16–22). Under the New Covenant, however, which is the Law of Love, we are protected against the temptation of the Pharisees. Our Law is inexhaustible, and it serves as much to reveal to us that we are sinners as it does to bring us closer to God.

–14–

WHAT IS A CHRISTIAN?

After John had been arrested, Jesus went into Galilee. There he proclaimed the Good News from God. "The time has come," he said, "and the kingdom of God is close at hand . . ." (Mark 1:14–20)

Many people who have been baptized think they are Christians because they have heard a great deal *about* Christ. The truth is that we are not Christians unless we have heard Christ *himself*; for the Word of Christ is like no other word that has ever been spoken. When we hear it, we recognize the voice that speaks it as the voice of our Master, and it makes us live as we have never lived before.

There are, of course, many reasons for believing. There are the five proofs of the existence of God; the miracles and the prophesies; the continued existence of the Church despite the arguments of her adversaries and notwithstanding the sins of her members; the ordered evolution of species toward more complex and improbable forms; and, finally, there is the need we all feel to find a meaning for life and death.

These are all conventional reasons for believing. But they do not add up, either individually or collectively, to faith. No more than a thousand objections necessarily constitute a single doubt.

There are many "witnesses to God" in the world today. Serious men and women who believe in all sincerity and who are committed to their faith. Yet, in a matter as important as faith, we are not always content merely to accept the testimony of others. We want to make certain for ourselves. We want witnesses who are sufficiently transparent for us to be able to see for ourselves what they are seeing.

What, then, is faith?

Essentially, it is the perception of the reality of the spiritual world. It is a personal, transforming encounter with the living Christ. We become Christians today, just as men did in the time of John the Baptist, by means of an interior witnessing of the Holy Spirit—a witnessing that enables us to recognize the presence, the voice, and the call of the Good Shepherd.

There are as many roads toward faith as there are men. And there are as many ways for God to make his voice heard as there are circumstances in life. But the privileged way is to hear the Word of God.

God speaks to man, and man feels a stirring at those levels within himself that are at once familiar and unknown to him. God himself reveals the level within us at which he manifests himself; and we are ignorant of that depth until he tells us of it. The certain sign that God is revealing himself is that he reveals us to ourselves; for only our Creator can know us and reveal us to ourselves in this way.

We hear for the first time, a voice that is somehow familiar. We know that it is not coming from outside ourselves; and we are certain that it is not our own voice. It speaks with quiet authority, like the voice of someone who *knows* and who speaks of a matter he has fully experienced. It calls to us from a different world, but a world that is capable of making all things clear in our world.

There are men and women who are converted by hearing a single sentence of the Gospels. What such persons experience cannot be explained, but it can be expressed as follows: "No one has ever spoken as this man speaks!"

Of course, our attitudes as we listen are important. We must listen quietly, without reticence and without being carried away by the experience. After all, it is not a matter of grasping a new concept, or of learning something, or of acquiring a new experience; for all these things are another way of tranquilizing our consciences by telling them that this is familiar ground for us. The Word itself helps to create the disposition necessary for us to hear what is being said, just as it unmasks the reasons we offer ourselves for not listening. "A child of God listens to the words of God," Jesus admonished the Pharisees. "If you refuse to listen, it is because you are not God's children" (John 8:47).

Thus, we have an infallible way of knowing if we are God's children or not. It is a test—a test we can give ourselves at every moment of our existence so as to recognize, for what they are, all of the detours, lies, and excuses that we offer ourselves to keep ourselves from listening to the Word. "The word of God is something alive and active," Saint Paul affirms. "It cuts like any double-edged sword but more finely. It can slip through the place where the soul is divided from the spirit, or joints from the marrow. It can judge the secret emotions and thoughts" (Hebrews 4:12).

The word of God is also a call. Those who belong to God hear it, and follow God. If a man does not hear it, it is because he does not belong to God. "Follow me," God says.

"Go where I tell you." And his voice reveals to us both our state of bondage and the possibility of being liberated from it. It removes our fetters and makes us tug at our chains.

Christian conversion always implies recognition of this kind. Even before the encounter with Christ, there is already a certain tendency toward faith; a sort of faith-before-faith, a love of truth and justice and mercy which makes us listen for the word of God. When we finally hear Jesus' call, we understand those things that we have done in darkness till then, and we open ourselves to the light and begin moving toward it with all possible speed.

"As I, who am sent by the living Father, myself draw life from the Father, so whoever eats me will draw life from me" (John 6:57). And "He who sent me is with me, and has not left me to myself, for I always do what pleases him." When Jesus had said this, John tells us (8:29), "Many came to believe in him." When they heard his words, the people entered into the intimacy of the Father and the Son. They became part of the delicate balance between modesty and pride, between equality and dependency, between tenderness and respect. And they knew that Jesus was the Son *par excellence*, and that he was indeed speaking to them of the Father.

Once a man has undergone such an experience, nothing can tear him away from the Father. His faith is then a personal conviction capable of overcoming any doubt or objection. Perhaps it cannot answer all doubts or triumph over all objections; but it can be relied upon not to deny under cover of darkness what it has seen in the light.

Since Vatican II, when the Church recognized that there was indeed abundant salvation outside of herself, many Christians have been troubled concerning their identity as Christians. What good does it do to be a Christian? How is a good Christian any better than a good atheist?

The reason that such questions are asked is that we have been reared in Christianity in exactly the same way as atheists have been reared in atheism; and this makes us surprisingly alike. For generations, the Church has kept Christians in the nursery and never led them to the personal encounter with Christ which she always preached. Christians believe what the Church says about Christ, and they think that their belief dispenses them from listening to Christ himself. They are able to repeat what they have learned in their catechisms, but they have never been able to verify, experience, and renew what they have learned.

How sad it is to find a Church whose witnesses all belong to the past. Today, more than ever, we need Christians who can say to the Church, as the Samaritans said to the Samaritan woman: "Now we no longer believe because of what you told us; we have heard him ourselves and we know that he really is the savior of the world" (John 4:42). We have need of Christians who are filled with wonder and go about saying, "Never has anyone spoken to me as this man has spoken! Never has anyone cured me, fed me, pardoned me, and raised me up as this man has!" We have need of Christians whom we can look at and say, "If it can happen to them, it can also happen to me. There must be a Presence, a mystery, a treasure hidden in this world, and my life will be changed once and for all as soon as I discover it."

-15-

THE JOY OF PENANCE

Repent, and believe the Good News. (Mark 1:15)

It seems a contradiction in terms to talk about the "joy of penance." Everyone knows that confession is a burden. It is something to be endured. And, for that reason, our confessionals are almost deserted. The confessional is the last place we look if we want a pleasant experience.

And yet, in the Gospels we find the Good News of the Kingdom constantly coupled with a call to repentance. The repentance in question is not an examination of conscience, but a conversion; not sadness at having sinned, but a celebration; not a verdict of guilty, but an announcement of pardon.

Far from making an inventory of his sins, the repentant sinner must turn to God and discover how much he has sinned by discovering how much he has ignored God's love, joy, and pardon.

Only God can ask us to repent, because only the one who forgives us can give us the strength to bear the sight of the evil we have committed—a sight that God reveals to us in forgiving that evil.

The Good News of the Kingdom is precisely this, that our sins *are* forgiven. Not that they *will be* forgiven if we fulfill certain onerous conditions. They are already forgiven. Pardon is already ours. All we have to do is to be willing to enter into a new world where punishment does not follow sin, where vengeance does not follow an offense, and where grace does not follow reparation—but precedes it.

We recognize our own sinfulness only by comparing ourselves to what we should be. We know ourselves only by knowing God. We know what we should be only by learning what God wants us to be. We know what we should have said in confession only when we leave the confessional, because we know our sins only by means of their forgiveness. We know what we were missing only when it is returned to us.

Christ was the great Liberator. He freed us not only from sin, but also from that whole universe of judgments, condemnations, debts, reparations, expiations, sadness, and shame which was part and parcel of sin. The experience of God's pardon was the experience of a liberation so total that only God could have effected it.

Human society is based upon a system of justice that includes courts, punishment, and prisons. Socially, we are still pagans in the sense that we believe that sin must be expiated before it can be forgiven. Christ, however, has revealed that a sin must be forgiven before reparation for it can be made.

For Christ, there is no life-force other than that of Love. A man does not begin to live until he begins to love. There is no greater waste than for a man to wait until he is grown before he discovers that he is worthy of being loved.

God's way is not a system of judgment and retribution. It is a system of creativity. It is not a system in which certain values are recognized and in which non-values are punished.

It is an order in which a man acknowledges that he is responsible for *creating* values.

Man sometimes makes mistakes about ideas, but ideas never mislead man. They lead him inexorably toward their logical consequences. Thus, men and human societies, grow to resemble the God they worship. If our society is so repressive, if it has so many judges, judgments, courts, and prisoners, it is because we have fashioned ourselves after the image we have of our God—a God "who judges the living and the dead." Instead of divinizing mercy and pardon, we have sacralized judges and judgment. We do not believe in the revolutionary truth of the Gospel: that sins are forgiven.

Our society is not a sign of God. Our courtrooms—whether or not they are decorated with the crucifix—are not a sign of God. Not even our confessionals are a sign of God. They are not "Good News." They are not an astonishment, a wonder, a joy. Our society recognizes and consecrates acquired values: money, prestige, honor, or unhappiness, poverty, humiliation, weakness. It ignores the Gospel, the Beatitudes, the dynamic transformation and revolution which is engendered by the forgiveness of sins.

We will become manifestations of God only if we take an interest in the poor, in sinners, in prisoners—in those whom we call "ex-convicts" but who remain isolated and paralyzed by the weight of their imprisonment. If we really believe that it is better to forgive than to punish, then we must break out of that vicious circle which makes us return evil for evil, punishment for sin, prison, for crime. We must preach the Gospel to the poor; and the Gospel, for all sinners, is nothing more than tremendous appeal to what is best in each of us.

Jesus spent his life honoring, respecting, and raising up

sinners. He recognized in each of them the child who did not mature for lack of sufficient love. He restored their innocence to them. He freed Zacheas from his greed, Mary Magdalene from her lovers, Matthew from his unfortunate profession. And his love—freely and generously given—made bloom in each of them that which all the world's justice would have stifled forever.

–16–

HOW DID JESUS PRAY?

. . . In the morning, long before dawn, he got up and left the house and went off to a lonely place and prayed there . . . (Mark 1:29–39)

When Jesus prayed, he did so in a way precisely like our own. Prayer for him, as for us, was not something automatic that he could turn on or off as he wished. He had to choose a place (the desert, the mountains, or some lonely place), the right moment, and circumstances that were appropriate for prayer.

This was no easier for Jesus than it is for us. He led a very busy life, and it was often difficult for him to find the time to pray. Even at the beginning of his public ministry, Mark tells us, it was necessary for Jesus to get up "long before dawn" in order to pray. Sometimes he went off by himself in the evening hours, or he stayed up at night. And occasionally, in order to have the quiet that is necessary to prayer, he had the Apostles take him out on a lake in their boat. It sometimes happened that even the presence of the Apostles disturbed Jesus; and then he would send them off to the other side of the lake on some improbable errand (Mark 6:45).

In spite of all these precautions, Jesus was apparently unable to enjoy any reasonable period of peaceful solitude.

There were always interruptions. People always wanted to see him. "Everybody is looking for you," the Apostles reported.

But Jesus did not allow his time to be monopolized, either by his friends or by his successes. He saw beyond such things, and he was eager to strike out in new directions. "Let us go elsewhere," he told the Apostles, "to the neighboring country towns, so that I can preach there too, because that is why I came."

What sort of prayer was it that Jesus was so anxious to protect? How could he, the Son of God, find it necessary to pray for some particular grace, or to ask for forgiveness?

Some theologians solved this problem (and protected Jesus' transcendence) by telling us that Jesus prayed merely to set an example for us; but that seems a farfetched explanation. Modern theologians generally have more respect for Jesus' real humanity and are more faithful to the Incarnation, and their explanations are more to the point. Father Duzoc, for example, states that "If Jesus' prayer has any meaning for us, if it can serve as an exemplar for our own prayers, it is because it had a meaning for Jesus himself."*

Jesus did not have such immediate access to divine knowledge and divine power as to be spared the dryness, darkness, and stops-and-starts that are natural to man. Jesus, like any other man, did not always enjoy the same clarity of view, or the same ability to concentrate. He was susceptible to distractions and outside influences. In order to think his thoughts and to meditate on what he knew, it was necessary for him to go "off to a lonely place."

He often left the crowds in a state of exasperation at their

* *Christologie*, p. 117.

disbelief. He was "grieved to find them so obstinate" (Mark 3:5) and impatient at their slowness to understand and their foolishness: "Have you no perception? Are your minds closed?" (Mark 8:17).

It was necessary for Jesus to withdraw in order to regain his calm and interior peace. He had to enter into himself so as to rediscover the nearness of the Father, the true meaning of his mission, his indulgence toward man, his faith in his power to redeem. Then he went out again to his friends, renewed, luminous, and serene.

Jesus was not exempt from temptation as the result of suffering, isolation, and fear. At such moments, he sometimes articulated what rose spontaneously to his lips: "My soul is sorrowful to the point of death . . . Father, everything is possible for you. Take this cup away from me" (Mark 14:34–37). These words were a manifestation of his human sensitivity. But through prayer he reflected and rediscovered his true nature. He was again aware of whence he came and where he was going. He was the Son once more, united to the Father; and then he had only one prayer: "Let it be as you, not I, would have it." And that is the Prayer of Jesus.

Is there really any other kind of prayer, even for us? Is there anything we can ask for that we have not already received? Surely the Father knows better than we do what we need and what is good for us. Is it possible for us to ask God for more than he is willing to give us? In fact, can we even ask God for something he has not already given us?

Prayer, then, is simply the act of becoming aware of God's gifts. It is remembering that we have a Father, that our Father has already given us whatever we could ask him for, and that he has given it more generously and lovingly than we could possibly expect him to. Therefore, when we pray insistently for something that we do not have, is it because we hope to wear down God's resistance to giving it? Or is it perhaps that we hope to wear down our own resistance to receiving?

The only true prayer for a Christian consists in imitating the prayer of Jesus. It is not a prayer of slaves and servants but of sons, full of confidence and assurance: "Father, I know that you always hear me! Father, I know that everything you have is mine!"

How long must we pray for the gift of praying like Jesus?

–17–

IS ANYONE OUT THERE PRAYING?

Simon, are you asleep? Had you not the strength to keep awake one hour? You should be awake, and praying not to be put to the test . . . (Mark 14:38)

Recently, a group of Christians asked me to conduct a retreat on prayer. Before the retreat itself, there was a meeting to establish the program, the subjects of the conferences, the time needed for discussion, for recreation, and so forth. When the meeting was breaking up, someone asked: "Tell me, are we actually going to pray during this retreat?"

There was an embarrassed silence. Every one of those who were organizing the retreat suddenly realized that he had long ago lost the habit of prayer. Finally, it was decided to consult with those who would be making the retreat and to suggest leaving time open for private meditation.

Not very long ago, priests prayed by reading their breviary, and laymen prayed by saying their rosary. Christians then measured their fervor by the regularity and length of these religious exercises.

Today, prayer presents a problem in theory as well as in practice. Not only do we not know *how* to pray; but we do not even know *if* we should pray. We do not know what prayer is, or what it means.

In the old days, people who did not pray were atheists, or Christians disgusted by the inefficacy of their prayers. Today, prayer has been abandoned for strictly religious reasons. There have been objections and criticism of traditional forms of prayer. There have been essays on improving those prayers, and translations of the prayers. And all this has led to an easily foreseeable consequence: no one prays any more.

Somehow, it all seems logical. We have learned that God has no need of our prayers to tell him what we need, since he knows better than we do what we must have. We have discovered that he cannot persuade God to do this or that for us, since he will do what is best for us in any case. Therefore, we have concluded that there is no use in praying.

There are some Christians who, in order to avoid this problem, refuse to allow any tampering with the traditional forms of prayer. The results are the same, however, for when we try to preserve everything we run the risk of destroying everything when a single error or a single weakness is discovered in that whole sacralized structure.

There is no doubt that some revision is necessary but, here as elsewhere, we run the danger of throwing out the baby with the bath water.

We should ask ourselves this question: What would prayer be like if it were purified of all its outdated forms? What are the stages through which we passed in our understanding and our practice of prayer?

Let us try to outline that evolution, beginning with the most commonplace formula:

(1) "Prayer is talking to God."

Fine. But what can we say to God? No doubt, we feel

the need to talk to God; but does God need to be talked to? What can we possibly tell him that he doesn't already know? We can talk, but our talking is a monologue that can continue only so long as we stay walled up within ourselves without really thinking about the one we are talking to. As soon as we raise our eyes to the one we are talking to, we stop thinking about what we are asking for and we can think about nothing except the one to whom we are addressing our requests. At that moment, we have nothing more to say, nothing more to ask. Once we have said, "Father," what more is there to say? At that moment, we must be quiet. We must trust God, not in a spirit of unhappy resignation, but in that of total openness to him. Jesus himself expressed a request in his prayer at Gethsemane, then canceled that request by giving preference to love.

(2) "Prayer is thinking about God with a feeling of love."

This makes a human activity of prayer; a loving soliloquy in which we do all the work. But our God is not a God who lets himself be loved and prayed to without answering. He is not the object of human activity and human yearning. Rather, God is the cause, the principle, the mover. What we call "contemplation" is not a Christian activity, for Christianity means participation. Prayer, therefore, is the moment when we consciously draw strength from the divine dynamism, from the eternal animation, that is always available to us.

(3) "To pray is to listen to God speaking to us."

The trouble with this definition is that God does not speak. In prayer, it is always man who speaks.

It is true, as some will object, that "God has spoken to us. We have the Gospels. We can listen to what he says." What we are forgetting is that these words of God are really the works of the men who listened to God—men like ourselves who listened as we do and who tried, as we do, to express what they heard. We can read those words as often as we wish; but they remain dead letters so long as we are not in direct communication with the same Spirit who inspired them long ago and who must give them new life today.

The fact is that God is silent, and it is up to us to interpret his silence. But just as there are empty words and meaningful words, so too there are meaningless silences and pregnant silences. The silence of God is full, rich, peopled, alive. When we listen to God's silence, we receive the power to make that silence fertile by interpreting it in the thousand ways available to us only at that level.

(4) "To pray is to try to say to God what God would say to us if he spoke. Prayer is listening to the echo of our words in God's silence. It is bringing our impulses face to face with the fundamental dynamism that animates us. It is bringing our interpretations to the source of their inspiration. It is listening with sufficient attention to know when to speak and when to remain silent. It is opening oneself to an inspiration. It is placing ourselves at the disposal of the One who summons us unceasingly."

At this level, there is no longer any distinction between a prayer of request and a prayer of praise, a prayer of repentance and a prayer of thanksgiving. There is only an awareness of what God whispers to us through events, through other men, and through our own ideals.

This discovery of the divine meaning of our lives, this perception of the "gift of God," can certainly be called a prayer of thanksgiving or of praise. God has given himself over entirely to mankind so that we may freely complete his work; and our communication with the inexhaustible energy of God is intended to make reparation with us for whatever we spoil without God.

Man, therefore, when he prays, should say everything he feels like saying, so that he may eventually say only that which is inspired by God.

Personally, I do not believe that prayer works on God or on events in the sense that it modifies the will of God. (Though I do believe that prayer may have a direct influence on people and things by means of an immediate psychic power.) But if prayer does not change God, it changes *us*, and it is we who are responsible for changing the world. Prayer places us in contact with our innermost strength and our most powerful resources, which consist in the creative inspiration of the Spirit. And that inspiration is capable endlessly of renewing the face of the earth.

God is not changed by prayer; but, in prayer, man opens himself to God's constant appeal. Man establishes a harmonious and effective relationship between himself and the world, between himself and others. And this relationship is impossible to those who do not pray.

We must pray, and we must pray always. But we must be aware that, in praying, we are not wearing down God's resistance to giving. It is our own resistance that we are wearing down: our resistance to receiving.

God in us is much more loving than loved, more serving

than served, more praying than prayed. We may therefore say that prayer is that moment when we listen to God so that we may change the world and change men. For God suffers from the world and from men infinitely more than we do.

–18–

GOD'S ORPHANS

My God, my God, why have you deserted me? (Mark 15:34)

It seems to me that the crucial question today, the question that tortures and divides contemporary Christians, consciously or unconsciously, is this: Where can we find God? Since the time when God was revealed through Jesus Christ, it seems that he has become more invisible than ever. God has been swallowed up in mankind to such an extent that it appears we can see him only in our brothers.

We should ask ourselves whether we truly have relations with God that do not coincide with our relations with other men. Is there really a way of building the Kingdom except by fighting for a human society in which justice and fraternal love prevail? Are our institutional religions anything more than superstructures, mythological interpretations of the great work of mankind as it evolves toward a destiny worthy of itself?

The absence and silence of God are a daily scandal to those few who still believe in him. We do not see God anywhere. He has no place in the scientific world, and scientists are proud that they no longer have need of God to explain empirical phenomena. God apparently is no longer indispensable even in the field of morals, for atheists have rules of conduct that are sometimes more rigorous and generous than those of Christians. God is no longer the foundation of the social and political order of the world. And he would discredit himself even further if, at this point, he demanded ritual worship, ceremonies, sacrifices; for today it is generally acknowledged that true greatness lies in simplicity, and that superiority consists in service.

Today, we see everywhere the confirmation of the words of Saint John: "No one has ever seen God" (1:18).

If that is so, then what is left of Christianity?

What is left is Christianity's essential doctrine: that Jesus preached, prepared, and lived the concept that a fully human life can be an authentic, full, divine life. For Jesus, there was no distinction between our relations with God and our relations with our fellow men. He told us not to expect heaven to intervene in our affairs in such a way as to relieve us of our human responsibilities and duties. God has already given us what we need in the way of gifts and knowledge. What remains is for us to do everything we can to discover what man is and to work so that we may become what we should be.

The two great instructions of Jesus that are the inspiration of modern theology are these:

(1) Matthew 25: "In so far as you did this to one of the least of these brothers of mine, you did it to me" (v. 40). God identifies himself with mankind and with every man. Therefore, our real relationship with God is not cultic, but social in nature. We are no closer to God than we are to our neighbors. We are no more agreeable to God than we are to our brothers. We will not be judged on the basis of our

religious practices, but on that of our familial, professional, and political conduct. We can be saved even if the thought of God has never crossed our minds: "Lord, when did we see you hungry and feed you; or thirsty and give you drink?" (v. 37). But we cannot be saved, regardless of our religious practices, unless we serve mankind.

(2) Mark 15, 34: "My God, my God, why have you deserted me?" Jesus cannot slip out of his human nature. He cannot use his divine power to save himself, as "religious" men try to do. His solidarity with mankind is total. He cannot count on God to intervene in order to save him. There is no "vertical" appeal from his fate. He can save himself—but only by saving us. And so, we know that no appeal to God can exempt us men from our human duties and responsibilities.

Obviously, it is not easy to believe that God has sent us such a message; that God himself has abolished "religion" and established humanism in its place; that God has annihilated himself in Jesus Christ—that is, that he has destroyed the ancient image that we had of him (and that we still have) in order to replace it with the image of a God who is human. How can we accept a God who is the most human of men and who teaches the rest of us how to be men?

It is much easier for us to distort the meaning of the incarnation and to believe that God only pretended to become man; that in reality he remained completely different from us and infinitely superior to us. For many Christians, Jesus was a mighty prince disguised as a beggar who, at a given moment, resumed the true identity for our edification and instruction. Throughout the Gospel narratives we can find little hints that the whole thing is somehow unreal. We find Jesus' birth dehumanized by a miraculous intervention. Jesus makes use of magical power to turn water into wine and to feed a crowd of people. Even Jesus' death is not a real death, for his corpse comes to life again.

Roger Garaudy, the eminent Marxist thinker, has put it very well: "We have stolen Christ from mankind," he said, "and turned him into a myth and a fairy tale."

The essential truth of Christianity is not that "God came down on earth," but that the only real image of God is contained in man himself. No matter how long we live and no matter how hard we try, we can never become sufficiently human to know God and to resemble him. It is therefore useless for us to try to imagine what God is like and to try to please him. Our goal should be to become men, to be members of an integral human community—as Jesus was.

It is true that God has disappeared; but he has done so only to reveal himself anew. God has deserted us only to make us discover him in our fellow men. If we look for him there, we will find him at the very moment we think we have lost him forever.

This is not an untested theory. It is the experience of many Christians active in politics, labor, and international affairs. These Christians began conventionally enough, out of religious motivations. But, as they became more and more absorbed in their work, they also became aware that their motives were changing. They had started out "for the love of God"; but they went on "for the love of man."

What they had lost was not God, but a superficial concept of the Incarnation. It was only when they felt that they were alone, that they were "orphans of God" and totally absorbed in their work, that they were really closest to Christ. Jesus was the first to experience that apparent estrangement from the Father at the very moment he was giving himself fully to mankind. It was at that moment that he made an act of faith which went beyond what he felt and united the two loves that filled his heart.

–19–

FEAR OF GOD AND BEING AFRAID OF GOD

. . . and the women came out and ran away from the tomb because they were frightened out of their wits; and they said nothing to a soul, for they were afraid. (Mark 16:1–8)

In our childhood, we were taught to be afraid of God. We were afraid even to think of God because such thoughts invariably awakened thoughts of God's anger and our own guilt. God was an eye—usually depicted as contained within a triangle—whose sole function was to watch us even when we were alone. God was a pitiless judge who would condemn us to eternal hellfire if we swallowed a drop of water before going to Communion, if we ate an ounce of meat on Friday, if we left out one sin in confession, or if we missed mass on a day of obligation. Our basic religious sentiment was a dread of mortal sin and a terror of hell; and our greatest ambition as Christians was to reach heaven as soon as possible without any accidents on the way.

Today, we wonder how we could have been so naïve. How could we have so misunderstood the Good News of God's mercy, God's forgiveness ("God is merciful," we were told, "but he is *also just*")? How could we have forgotten Jesus' tenderness toward sinners and ignored the freedom of God's children?

It is true that being afraid is a powerful incentive to discipline. To be afraid of "God is the beginning of wisdom," the Psalmist tells us. And our religious education usually stopped at that beginning. Apparently, it was felt that being afraid was enough to keep us within the proper limits.

The grip of terror in which we were held was not easily shaken. The evidence of it is still with us. We often hear grown men speak with great independence of religious practices and refer to them disparagingly as "superstitions"—but those same men would never dare miss their Easter duties.

Certainly, if we scare children sufficiently with the threat of eternal punishment, we can be more or less certain that they will never miss Sunday mass. And we can be equally sure that they will never love God.

Fear is a sign of lack of love and lack of faith. What mother or father worthy of the name would not be ashamed of making their children afraid of them?

God is our Father, and the Gospels are filled with the refrain: "Do not be afraid!" It begins with the Annunciation and it ends with the apparitions of the Risen Christ. When the Apostles were gathered together and Jesus suddenly stood among them, they were filled with "alarm and fright" because "they thought they were seeing a ghost" (Luke 24:37–38). And Jesus' first words to them were words of mercy and joy: "Peace be with you" (Luke 24:37) and "There is no need for alarm" (Mark 16:6).

It is time to ask ourselves whether we are afraid of God or whether we fear God. It is a sin to be afraid of God. It offends him as a Father, and it is a trick of the devil to dissuade us from loving God.

The fear of God, however, is a gift of the Holy Spirit, a sign of love, a refinement of the heart.

To be afraid of God means that we think God will do us harm, punish us, send misfortune down upon our heads, send us to hell. But the fear of God is born of the discovery that God is so good, so gentle, so vulnerable that *we* can hurt *him.*

The whole of Christian revelation consists in the astonishing news that God cannot harm us, but that we can injure him. Compare this to the pagan belief, in which we were reared, that God is powerful, invulnerable, untouchable, immutable; that he judges us, threatens us, and punishes us.

The atheist who rejects a vengeful and oppressive God is more Christian in his heart than a Christian who accepts such a God. Christians who think they worship God often worship nothing more than strength. But Jesus revealed the weakness of God. God is weak because God is Love, and love makes us humble, gentle, poor, and vulnerable with respect to those we love.

The true face of God is manifested not in power and glory, but in humility and suffering. Mankind was expecting a judge, a sword, an executioner. Instead, a child was born. This child held out his arms to the world and asked: "Do you want me?"

Man answered: "I'm not worthy! I'm a sinner. I'm not good enough."

"What does that matter?" the child asked. "I'm here to forgive sins. I don't care about what happened in the past. Do you want me?"

Everyone hesitated, as we ourselves hesitate today. Can

God really be as weak as all that? people wondered. Is it actually possible that God can be as helpless, as open, as trusting, as innocent as a child?

What, after all, is a young child? It is a being to whom we can do anything we want without having to be afraid that he will revenge himself. In other words, a child is the exact opposite of the terrible idol that we built for ourselves in place of God. And what could be more necessary or more urgent than that God reveal himself to us as he really is?

The other face God shows to us is that of Jesus crucified; and this face, like that of the child, is one of helplessness. A man, when he is crucified, has his hands nailed to the cross. He cannot strike out at his tormentors. His feet are nailed to the cross, so he cannot kick. A crucified man, like a child, is a being to whom we can do anything we want without having to be afraid that he will fight back.

When we look upon the crucified Christ, we should be struck by the fact that it is he rather than we who is weak, humble, dependent. In comparison to him, we are strong and free. We are more "God" than he.

The Christ who urges us in the Gospels not to be afraid is the same Christ who, in the face of our discouragements and apprehensions, surprises us by his gentleness, his willingness to forgive, and his invitation to hope. He is still the Crucified. He is still vulnerable. But he is also as benevolent and kind to us as we have been cruel to him.

–20–

THE SIN AGAINST THE HOLY SPIRIT

> *. . . I tell you solemnly, all men's sins will be forgiven, and all their blasphemies; but let anyone blaspheme against the Holy Spirit, and he will never have forgiveness: he is guilty of an eternal sin.* (Mark 3:20–29)

The Good News of the Gospel, as we know, is the proclamation of God's free, indiscriminate, and joyful forgiveness of our sins. It is a forgiveness accorded without condition and without the necessity for penance—except the penance of accepting that forgiveness and allowing it to transform us.

Yet, in the third chapter of Mark, we read that there is an unforgivable sin: an "eternal sin." After the announcement of the Good News, is it possible that there really is a sin that God is unwilling to forgive?

Like anything that is written or spoken, Jesus' words can be understood properly only if they are taken within their context. We must remember that the Old Testament describes the reign of the Father as he revealed himself in nature and in the history of the Jews. This revelation was provisional and progressive, and it influenced comparatively few people. What remains, after a reading of the Bible, is an impression of a God who is little understood, a Father who has been rejected, a Spouse who has been betrayed.

The New Testament, on the other hand, is an account of the reign of the Son. But the Son's glory is hidden while he is on earth. It appears clearly only after the Ascension. The Son, too, disappoints, discourages, and irritates his fellow citizens, his partisans, his family, and his disciples. Even his Precursor finally feels obliged to ask him outright: "Are you the one who is to come, or must we wait for someone else?" (Luke 7:19).

Finally, there came the era of the Church, which is the reign of the Holy Spirit. And this represents God's supreme and definitive effort to manifest himself to us. There can be no fourth era, any more than there can be a fourth person in the Trinity. If anyone is not convinced by the testimony of the Holy Spirit, then there is no hope for such a man to be saved. By waiting for a new revelation from God, we lay ourselves open to the snares of the anti-Christ who will rally around himself all those who think that God should have made himself known through force, fear, money, discipline, and organization rather than through Love.

According to the Gospels, there is nothing more visible, more audible, more tangible than the Holy Spirit; and those who refuse to recognize the presence of the Spirit show that they are irreversibly closed to God.

Jesus himself told us that it was expedient for him to leave us so that he might send the Holy Spirit to us; and it was the Spirit who would convert the entire world.

Later, when Saint Peter, on the feast of Pentecost, spoke to the pagans about the Holy Spirit, he did not tell them what they must believe, but what they *saw* and *heard:* "Now raised to the heights by God's right hand, he has received from the Father the Holy Spirit, who was promised, and what you see and hear is the outpouring of that Spirit" (Acts 2:33).

But what did they see and hear? The Holy Spirit, like the Son, is incarnated and shows himself only through the intermediary of men. When the people saw the Apostles and witnessed their joy, their self-assurance, their understanding, and their new-found audacity, they must have realized that the Master was now living in them; that the Apostles had gone through a kind of resurrection of their own, and that the Spirit of Jesus was more alive than ever.

In the early centuries of the Christian era, when a man had to be chosen for an important mission, the people looked for someone "filled with the Holy Spirit." That is, a man who radiated a spirit of love, faith, gentleness, and peace. The presence of the Holy Spirit in such a man was visible, tangible, and no one could deny that presence.

Even more than individuals, however, the Holy Spirit manifested himself in human relationships within a community; for nothing is more visible than a spirit of love. When there is love among members of a family, the fact is immediately obvious to everyone. And when love is lacking, what could be more evident? How is it possible to hide such a thing? In the face of such emptiness, our first instinct is to flee—an instinct that parents themselves recognize when they say: "I don't know what's wrong, but the children are never at home."

The witness borne by love is so visible, so eloquent and persuasive that it is able to convert the world. The pagans said of the first Christians: "*See* how they love one another!"

To establish a true Church, to build a living community,

is to make God visible and present in the world. "Where two or three people are gathered in my name, I am there with them." The meaning is clear: where a love is alive, there also lives the Spirit of Jesus; and that Spirit is as visible as love itself.

We hear a great deal today about God's absence and about the death of God. What is missing, however, is not God, but the Spirit of Love; and we ourselves are responsible for that lack. The Spirit has not stopped offering himself to us, but we have stopped welcoming him. In so doing, we not only deprive the world of the sight of God which it needs, but we also mortally weaken our own faith which cannot survive without the living testimony of love.

Our huge churches, cold and impersonal as they are, are not habitations of the Holy Spirit even when they are filled with Christians. The faithful are not united there, but merely juxtaposed. Their mutual indifference precludes any exchange among them; and therefore the Holy Spirit, Love, is not made visible. Is there a single instance of anyone being converted at Sunday mass?

It is useless to hope that the world will be converted to God until mankind is given the opportunity to see a true Church. Men will never be converted by proofs, demonstrations, and syllogisms. They have been too often deceived by propaganda in the past. They have believed in too many gods and have suffered too many disappointments. Young people, particularly, are determined not to be taken in by lies and publicity campaigns. They will believe only what they can *see*. They must see the Holy Spirit, hear him, and touch him before they will believe that he is real.

This is precisely the kind of evidence that the first Christians offered to unbelievers. When the dissolute pagan world was given the opportunity to observe the innocence, joy, and fraternal love that prevailed in Christian communities, it suddenly realized that there was truly a spirit capable of renewing and transforming human life.

In our own time, in a world divided and disfigured by hate, racism, drugs, and violence, the only hope lies in the witness borne by Christian communities in which there is life, faith, and love.

It is easy to convert the world. All we have to do is make the Holy Spirit visible.

– 21 –

MARY AND US

Who are my mother and my brothers? (Mark 3:33)

In the past several years, there has been a profound reaction against what is described as excessive devotion to Mary. Vatican II disappointed the hopes of certain "Mariolaters" by its discretion in this respect. The conciliar fathers even refused to accord Mary the title of "Mother of the Church."

The Council's prudence was motivated by the exigencies of the ecumenical movement. In the interests of Christian unity, it seems wise for Catholics not to insist on emphasizing a devotion that many Protestants find offensive. Uncontrolled piety and an overly speculative theology have made Mary a subject of discord among Christians, whereas, as a Mother, her role should be to unite us.

Today, we pride ourselves on adhering to essentials; on going straight to the heart of the matter. We do not want to linger over non-essentials. And the essential questions, it seems, are those of belief and non-belief in God, of transcendence and Immanence, of the Vertical and the Horizontal, of God and Man.

It is also true that the more skeptical we are at a particular point in history, the more dangerous it is to encourage forms of secondary devotion. In an age of faith, even the most naïve religious practices somehow come to life; they are rendered authentic by the vigor of man's faith. But when faith is weak, special devotions are like veins emptied of blood. They harden, are isolated from the rest of the system, and become detrimental to it. Thus, the general lack of faith today threatens to make certain manifestations of piety, which once were useful and touching, appear to be mere superstitions. We have so little faith, it seems, that we must reserve what we have for the essentials.

The apparent eclipse of devotion to Mary is actually an opportunity for Christians to return to the sources of their faith. Our era is much taken with a return to the Scriptures; and the most authentic and fertile source for true devotion to Mary is—the Gospels. When Catholics reread the Gospels (if indeed they have ever read them before), they are often astonished to discover the humanity, freshness, and sensitivity with which the Evangelists speak of Mary. (In considering these texts, we would do well to abstract from the marvelous and the miraculous; for the reading of Scripture is more rewarding when we are able to see our own lives in the light of the Gospel, and the Gospel in the light of our own lives.)

In reading the description of the Annunciation, for instance, we discover, like a rich lode of precious ore, the story of our own vocations. Remember that nowhere is it said that Mary actually "saw" an angel. She simply received a message: a mission from God, just as we do every day of our lives when we are attentive to the calls we receive. For God must come into the world every day. Christ is born continually and he grows constantly. The greatest adventure that is possible for us is to take the Gospel seriously.

Luke (1:26–38) reveals to us that Mary's reaction to this

message was exactly what ours would be: she asked herself what its meaning could be. She questioned. She was "deeply disturbed." The dialogue with the angel recounted by Luke is a literary dramatization of a natural process of deliberation; a deliberation that took place, as it does for us, in time and over a period of time, for the presence of the Spirit of God is never discerned instantly. Apparently, Mary read the Scriptures in an effort to understand what was happening to her, for the Magnificat is filled with quotations highly appropriate to Mary's circumstances. And then Mary sought advice from a person of some experience, her cousin Elizabeth.

Mary was not immediately filled with joy at her vocation. She did not celebrate as soon as her mission was made known to her. Instead, like each one of us, she was depressed, overwhelmed, and astonished. It was only after she arrived to visit Elizabeth that it all became clear to her and that she exclaimed: "My soul proclaims the greatness of the Lord!" (Luke 1:46). It had happened in the same way for Elizabeth, who achieved understanding only gradually, after being told that she herself would bear a child in her old age. "For five months," Luke records, "she kept to herself" after having conceived (1:24).

Despite the bond of humanity that exists between Mary and us, there is much in devotion to Mary that irritates modern man (and, perhaps even more, modern woman): the exaggerations, the hyperbole, the extraordinary privileges and titles. One could almost say that the Church tried to compensate for its traditional and practical oppression of women by exalting the ideal of womanhood as personified in Mary. That exaltation, however, has led us, especially in the twentieth century, to say: "If God could make such exceptions in order to turn out a human being who was completely pleasing to him, why didn't he do the same thing for all of us? After all, Mary was given the privilege of the Immaculate Conception, the divine maternity, a superabundance of graces of all sorts, impeccability—and only God knows what else. Obviously, her life was much easier than ours. We don't have her privileges or the kind of head-start she had."

There is some truth in that objection. But the whole truth is that it is the theologians, and not the Evangelists, who have emphasized the things in which we differ from Mary. The Gospels insist on those aspects in which we are *like* Mary; and it is for this reason that reading the Gospels, unlike reading the theologians, is so stimulating to Marian devotion. What contemporary man or woman does not feel that Mary was a kindred spirit when he reads texts like the following:

> "She was deeply disturbed by these words and asked herself what this greeting could mean" (Luke 1:29).
>
> "I am the handmaid of the Lord" (1:38).
>
> "The child's mother and father stood there wondering at the things that were being said about him" (2:33).
>
> "They were overcome when they saw him" (2:48).
>
> "They did not understand what he meant" (2:50).

Which of us would not scold our own children as Mary did Jesus: "My child, why have you done this to us? See how worried your father and I have been, looking for you" (2:48).

And what mother would not do as Mary did at the end:

"Near the Cross of Jesus stood his mother . . ." (John 19:25).

If we were looking for the single piece of spiritual advice that we could put to best use in our daily lives, we could not do better than choose to do as Mary did: "They did not understand what he meant . . . [but] his mother stored up all these things in her heart"—which is to say that she meditated upon them (Luke 2:50–52).

In meditating what Jesus says in the light of our own lives and experiences, we discover a Mary who was by no means a stranger to the doubts, suffering, and lack of understanding that constitute our daily lives. And we also discover one who is able to teach us to attain the same acceptance, the same submission, and the same faith which she attained. In other words, we will find the woman who is truly our Mother.

–22–

DEATH AND RESURRECTION

. . . *The child is not dead, but asleep.* . . . (Mark 5:35–43)

"Why are the heroes of your novels always so full of anguish?" a journalist once asked Françoise Sagan.

"Because," the novelist replied, "they live with the thought of death."

And André Malraux once remarked that "Man is the only animal who knows that he is mortal."

Truly, one is not a man unless he is conscious of the great mystery of death, and even if he does not succeed ever in resolving that mystery, unless he comes to terms with it.

The mystery of death envelops not only the phenomenon of death itself, but also what lies beyond death. Even if we admit the existence of a hereafter of some kind, there remains the scandal of our complete ignorance regarding the future life, and the scandal of our total separation from those who have died.

The fact seems to be that we are confined within some kind of terrestrial prison, and that this imprisonment frustrates our noblest aspirations. At a given moment, we run into a stone wall, and everything we hold dear, our most vital relations, are reduced to nothingness in an instant.

We say that love is stronger than death. And yet, death inexorably separates those who love one another and refuses to allow us the consolation of the slightest sign of life or love from beyond the grave. We can continue to love one who has died, of course; but we cannot communicate with him in any way. And what is love without communication, without the hope ever of seeing the one we love?

How easily we understand the motivations of Orpheus, who risked his own life to rescue Eurydice from the realm of death. But we must remember that as soon as Orpheus tried to communicate with Eurydice after finding her, she was lost to him again.

How easy it is for us to sympathize with those who believe in metempsychosis—the transmigration of souls. Such people at least live their lives and preserve their dead in a familiar universe. But if the survival of a soul is unconscious, what good does it do? And, since we are ourselves only by virtue of our consciousness of ourselves, how can we say that it is really *we* who survive after death in metempsychosis?

How easy it is to understand the thinking of those who attempt to enter into communication with the dead through spiritualism—except that the "messages" received from beyond are usually so vague and disappointing that silence would seem preferable to communication of this sort.

When we come face to face with the insurmountable barrier of death which surrounds us, we can understand the state of mind of those who are tempted to rebel. But it is useless to rebel against something we do not understand. To rebel against something is to reject something; but if we do not understand what we want to rebel against, then, instead of rebelling, we should continue our search for understanding.

The absurd and the mysterious are not the same thing. The absurd is that which has no meaning and cannot have a meaning; but a mystery is something that has more meaning than we have understanding.

The problem, if one tries to express it simply, is this: Why is it that we know nothing about the other life? Why is it that we have no communication with those who have died? And wouldn't it be easier to believe that death means extinction, annihilation, rather than to believe that those who have died are now indifferent to us and ignore us?

These are questions that Christ never answers. Instead of answering, Christ acts. Jesus never explains. He lives, and he gives life. He hints that he knows the secret of a life that is stronger than death; that something of man survives death just as consciousness somehow survives during sleep. For death, like sleep, resembles annihilation, but for both there is an awakening which gives the lie to that similarity.

The essential factor that Jesus introduces is his absolute faith in the omnipotence of love. Jesus is a free man, the only truly free man, the only man who has loved and believed with sufficient daring both to free himself from fear, from money, from habit, from the law, and from death, and to free others from the same things. To encounter Christ is to be subjected to a violent appeal to free oneself. "Do not be afraid," was Jesus' first recommendation to Jairus in this narrative of Mark's. "Have faith!" (5:36). He taught that if a man had a little faith, he would be delivered from slavery in all its forms. And when Jesus' listeners believed him, when his contagious freedom infected them to the point that they experienced a sense of freedom for the first time, they then discovered that nothing was impossible to him. The sick were freed of their infirmities, the greedy were liberated from their love for money, the lustful were freed from the needs of their flesh, the sinners regained their innocence, and even the dead were restored to life.

Jesus restored man to the state in which he had originally been created. For the first time it was possible to understand why man had been created and to perceive the splendor of God's plan. It was revealed that man could be free, that he could become like God. It was now possible to love man by seeing him as God saw him; and it was possible to love God by seeing his image in man. Man was filled with a great joy. He could begin to live! The world he had known before Jesus' coming was as nothing compared to that which Jesus had revealed. And the man who dared to believe and to love as Jesus did, like Jesus could transform the world.

The raising to life of the daughter of Jairus, described in the fifth chapter of Mark (35–43), was the life-size representation of what every man felt happening within himself when he came into contact with the Great Liberator. It was a precise explanation of that startling proposition which caused some to flee in panic and others to be catalyzed. When Jesus raised the daughter of Jairus from the dead, it was *our* resurrection that he was enacting. Jesus was offering to raise us up immediately, while we are still alive. "The child is not dead, but asleep," he said.

And the resurrection he proposed to work in us was no less startling, and no less life-giving, than that which he performed for the daughter of Jairus.

Jesus did not make mere promises. He did not talk about a future life. He dealt with immediate reality in such a striking way that one could see, with astonishment, how few people actually wished to live that life, how few actually wished to be so raised up from the dead. "They laughed at him," Mark says. "So he turned them all out . . . and taking the child by the hand he said to her, 'Talitha, kum!' which means, 'Little girl, I tell you to get up.' The little girl got up at once and began to walk about . . ." (5:40–42).

It was only when the Apostles began to believe in their own resurrection that they began also to believe in the resurrection of Christ. It was necessary for them to die to their ambitions and prejudices and pessimism before they could be raised up in the faith, joy, and fearlessness of Jesus. They knew that Jesus was alive in themselves only when they felt themselves filled with the freedom of Jesus.

-23-

STRANGE RETRIBUTION

The man who has will be given more: from the man who has not, even what he has will be taken away. (Mark 4:25)

These are hard words, shocking words to hear from Jesus. They seem to contradict everything in the Magnificat. Taken in their literal sense, they constitute a cynical summing-up of the Marxist belief in the concentration of goods in the hands of the capitalists and the gradual proletarization of the masses.

It is fashionable nowadays for both Marxists and Christians to affirm their solidarity with "the poor" and to declare their determination to free the poor from their poverty. And now, here is Jesus himself apparently telling them both that they are wrong and, at the same time, putting the seal of divine approval on the inequitable distribution of wealth.

Obviously, that is not at all what Jesus really meant. There are kinds of wealth which damn those who try to preserve them; and the Gospel curses the rich by saying that all that they have tried to store up will be taken away from them. Also, we read that the poor are blessed, for theirs is the Kingdom.

The possessions that Jesus is talking about in this text are of a different kind. He is referring to values that cannot be passed on from one man to another. The habit of prayer is one such value. It is difficult to acquire; but, once acquired, we can increase it enormously. The habit of recollection, of being open to others, of being at the disposal of God and our fellow men, of fighting for justice, of being generous—all these things are values that increase through faithful practice in those who possess them, but eventually become impossible to those who, over a long period of time, reject them.

Certainly, we have an obligation to place everything we have at the service of others. If we are talking about money, then it is easy to get others to accept it. But if we are talking about one's indifference to money, then we are dealing with a value that is indeed difficult to communicate to another. In the spiritual and moral order, there are no beggars and no profiteers. We are all poor men who must work in order to live.

The Fathers of the Church were well aware of the radical distinction between material wealth and spiritual riches. Material wealth is that which we desire greatly when we do not have it, but which, once possessed, quickly leads to satiety. To induge excessively in food or drink, for instance, can entail sufferings that are not much easier to endure than those caused by lack of sufficient food or drink.

Spiritual riches, on the other hand, are not desired by anyone who does not already possess them. They are so alien, in fact, that we are not even aware that we lack them. Of course, a man who has no faith, who does not pray, who does not love—such a man senses vaguely that something is missing from his life. But most often he believes that the cure for his unease lies in money, or power, or even in increased activity. He has no way of knowing that these "cures" will cause him to lose the bit of peace, love, and conscience he may still possess. But the man who has tasted spiritual wealth will never have his fill of them, and he will spend his life in search of them.

"The man who has will be given more; from the man who has not, even what he has will be taken away." These words of Jesus, severe as they are, do not express a judgment of God. They are only a statement of fact; a warning of the end to which human perversity can lead. God gives, offers, proposes to every man until the very end; but man is capable of refusing God's gifts, offers, and proposals until the last—even though his refusal involves his own self-destruction.

Cardinal Newman tells us that what most shocked him when assisting at the deathbeds of non-believing friends was the opposition between a supreme proposition and a refusal so strong that it virtually constituted an inability to accept. It was as though these persons were aware that they were about to lose, permanently, a presence that had given their lives whatever fruitfulness and warmth they possessed, but to which they had nonetheless always refused to open themselves.

We have all known people who live in a state of permanent refusal with respect to a love, a goodness, a tenderness, a mercy that is always offered to them and unceasingly nourishes and sustains them, but which they make it a point of honor to resist.

Man's capacity for refusal truly surpasses belief!

The moment of a man's death is of supreme importance precisely because he is finally brought to the point where he *must* make a choice. Until then, it is possible for him to refuse and, simultaneously, to keep that which he has refused. But when a man who thinks he has "nothing" is about to die, the moment has arrived when he is in danger of losing even that little which he has.

There is, in this situation, a source of infinite hope for those who love and are not loved in return. A great number of people refuse to open themselves to love; but, at the same time, they would be unable to exist without that against which they struggle so unceasingly.

We must never forget the warning implicit in Jesus' words. It is entirely possible that by persistent refusal and denial we will one day succeed finally in destroying that which has always sustained us, in expelling that which has always been a source of life to us.

"But," says Saint Paul, "who can ever separate us from the love of Christ? Isn't it always available to us?"

–24–

GOD'S INCOGNITO

> *... And Jesus said to them, "A prophet is only despised in his own country, among his own relations and in his own house"; and he could work no miracle there . . . he was amazed at their lack of faith.* (Mark 6:1–6)

For thirty years, Jesus lived like everyone else. He lived in a village with his family, with his mother, his "brothers" and his "sisters." He did what everyone else did. He played, ate, worked, talked, prayed; and no one took any special notice of him.

During this period Jesus was not in hiding. If his life was hidden, in any sense of that term, man's blindness and natural insensitivity is enough to explain it without our having to attribute it to any particular intention on Jesus' part.

Jesus' humble existence with his fellow men was the revelation of the true God: God living at ease in the little house of Mary and Joseph; God daily expressing himself by words and gestures; and God filling the most ordinary words, the simplest relations, the most ordinary life, with love. In such a life is reflected the unbelievable depth of the mystery contained in every life, the secret hidden within those most familiar to us, the inscrutability and incommunicability of those whom we encounter every day of our lives.

To superficial observers like ourselves, the people we know are all vaguely alike in most respects. Mankind appears to us like a great city, seen from afar at night. The blazing lights offer excitement, the lure of the unknown. But as we enter the city, we see that it is not unlike every other city we know. As we speed through the streets, we glimpse domestic scenes and dramas that seem commonplace and ordinary. The lives of the people appear to be the same as everyone else's. There is nothing individual or different about them. And yet, to someone who truly *loves,* each of those lives is unique, irreplaceable, marvelous, and inexhaustible.

What a strange creature man must be for God to feel it is necessary sometimes to reveal himself so clearly and at other times to hide himself so completely. The Gospel tells us that Jesus' contemporaries were just like us. Like them, we take no notice of the very presence we are looking for so frantically everywhere around us.

Man is a bottomless well. In his depths, both good and evil abound. But man is judged not by what he contains. He is judged by the kind of discovery he makes. Even Jesus could work no miracles at Nazareth because of the lack of faith of the people there. Everywhere else, the manifestation of God in the power of Jesus' love awakened the admiration and wonder of the people and, simultaneously, awakened the admiration of Jesus himself for the trust and faith of the people. "Your faith has saved you," Jesus said.

It is very easy for us to tell ourselves that our generosity is limited only by the shortcomings of our neighbors. We are unwilling to recognize that the limitation exists not in our neighbors but in ourselves. If we were more perceptive, more aware, we would have gone far beyond the point at which we stopped in disappointment. Nietzsche once said: "If only man's love for woman, and woman's love for man, were the pity that two disguised, suffering gods feel for each other! But, almost always, it is nothing more than one animal catching the scent of another."

In everyone we meet, in every one of the people around us, there is a disguised God waiting for us to discover him so that he can show himself to us as he is. Faith and love give sight. We must believe and love in order to be able to see clearly. Habit, however, blinds us, and there is no worse blindness than that which makes us unable to see those whose presence is routine. We no longer look at such people; and that is even worse than never having seen them at all, for it means that we will *never* see them. If a man is ignorant, it is still possible for him to learn. But if a man who is ignorant believes that he knows everything, he will never learn anything at all. In the same way, a man who does not believe can always be converted; but a man who thinks that he believes is doomed to remain an unbeliever.

Faith and love are the leaven that quicken our existence. Great quantities of this leaven are necessary in the most ordinary life for it merely to be bearable. And it is evident that very few of our contemporaries find their lives bearable.

We ask ourselves: How could the people of Nazareth not have recognized Jesus for what he was? Instead, let us ask ourselves this question: If the Savior of the world turned out to be a member of our own family, or one of our coworkers, or a neighbor of ours, would we be willing to recognize him as such? Would we love him, revere him, listen to him? Would we have been sufficiently aware of those around us not to be astonished at the sudden revelation?

The Gospel emphasizes our enormous responsibility for ourselves. No miracles can be worked unless we receive the miracleworker with love and faith. If we want the Savior of the world to appear and to grow among us, we must live as though we expect him every day and every moment of our lives.

-25-

WHAT IS CLEAN AND WHAT IS UNCLEAN?

> *. . . Nothing that goes into a man from outside can make him unclean; it is the things that come out of a man that make him unclean. . . .* (Mark 7: 1–23)

It is difficult for us twentieth-century Christians to realize the great shock, not to say the scandal, that Jesus' words caused among his contemporaries. Everyone, pagan and Jew alike, lived in a world hedged in by countless taboos. Objects and foods were either clean or unclean, sacred or profane, benevolent or malevolent. And anyone who violated one of these mysterious taboos invited terrible retribution.

Bishop Zoa, an African convert to Catholicism, has given us an account of what he felt on the day of his baptism. His pagan education had filled him with superstitious fears, and he had spent his youth in a world of terror, believing that such and such a sign was evil, or that this or that day was unlucky. He was convinced that if he walked under a certain tree, he would be struck dead; if he drank from a certain well, he would become sterile; if he did not pronounce a certain incantation correctly, misfortune would befall him. The moment of his baptism was the moment that set him free.

Then, consecrated by Christ, he dared confront the terrors of his childhood. He violated the old taboos and experienced the triumphant freedom of a child of God. On that day, he walked in the jungle like a new Adam strolling in Paradise. He had been reconciled to the universe. Christ had demolished all barriers. No longer was anything or anyone clean or unclean by nature or by birth. Cleanliness came from a man's heart, and all things were good if they were used for good. Only sin made things unclean.

Saint Peter described a similar experience in which Christ overcame the Apostle's hereditary prejudices. Peter, in ecstasy, ". . . saw heaven thrown open and something like a big sheet being let down to earth by its four corners; it contained every possible sort of animal and bird, walking, crawling, or flying ones. A voice then said to him, 'Now, Peter; kill and eat!' But Peter answered, 'Certainly not, Lord; I have never yet eaten anything profane or unclean.' Again, a second time, the voice spoke to him, 'What God has made clean, you have no right to call profane'" (Acts 10:10–15).

This vision of Peter's prepared him for his meeting with Cornelius, the Roman centurion. For it was not only objects and animals that were regarded as "unclean," but also some men—and all women. "You know," Peter said, "it is forbidden for Jews to mix with people of another race and visit them, but God has made it clear to me that I must not call anyone profane or unclean" (Acts 10:28).

The incarnation of Christ abolished the natural distinction between profane and sacred and between unclean and clean. Jesus desacralized everything that had been sacred; and he sacralized man—all men. "Your bodies are the Temple of the Holy Spirit," Saint Paul assures us.

Thenceforth, that which is truly sacred—i.e., God—is offered to all men and permeates all men to the extent that they allow it to do so. We should recall the stupefaction of the Jewish believers when they saw "that the gift of the Holy Spirit should be poured out on the pagans too, since they could hear them speaking strange languages and proclaiming the greatness of God. Peter himself then said, 'Could anyone refuse the water of baptism to these people, now they have received the Holy Spirit just as much as we have?' " (Acts 10:45–47).

Often there is not much difference between the old ways and our own. We, too, have our taboos—taboos that Christ abolished but that we have attempted to preserve. And these are not only the simple superstitions that are so common among both believers and unbelievers—spilling salt, breaking a mirror, walking under a ladder, or knocking on wood. We have also attributed to certain objects that sacred character that belongs only to man himself.

Many of us remember the days when it was considered a serious sin for a layman to touch the chalice. As though a Christian were not infinitely more sacred than a metal cup, and infinitely more worthy of receiving his God than a chalice was of containing that God!

There are even places where husbands and wives still regard their sexual relations as "impure"—so much so that they will not receive the Eucharist the morning after sexual contact. Yet, Jesus said: "It is from within, from men's hearts, that evil intentions emerge . . ." (Mark 7:21).

One of the most difficult taboos to lay to rest is that which has it that women are somehow "unclean." Women still are not allowed to enter the sanctuaries of our churches, to serve at Mass—let alone to become priests. Women, it is still felt, attain dignity only through virginity; that is, by denying their sexuality—as though there were some irreconcilable opposition between a woman's sexuality and her dignity.

Another of our revered superstitions is expressed in our astonishment when we see holiness or spiritual genius flourish elsewhere than in the Church "outside of which there is no salvation." We Christians have long believed that we have a monopoly of the Holy Spirit. Certainly, if the Spirit's activities were confined to Catholics, we would have to admit that he is a rather ineffectual Spirit. Fortunately, however, the Spirit has the universe as his field of operation. He enlightens every man who comes into the world. Every man who is of the truth hears the voice of the Spirit. Every man who loves justice is born of the Spirit. Every man who loves, is born of God and knows God.

God regards no man as "unclean." He does not fear contamination from any of us. He stands at the heart of every man, waiting to be admitted. "Look, I am standing at the door, knocking. If one of you hears me calling and opens the door, I will come in and share his meal, side by side with him" (Revelation 3:20).

–26–

ON BEING THE GREATEST

. . . *If anyone wants to be first, he must make himself last of all and servant of all.* . . . (Mark 9:30–37)

There was no teaching of Christ's that the Apostles resisted more obstinately than that of his humiliation and his Cross. The Gospel presents us with a dramatic re-enactment of that opposition between God's way and man's.

Jesus had just confided his most intimate thoughts to his disciples, his growing certitude that he would suffer and be put to death, his total trust in the love of the Father. "But they did not understand what he said," Mark records. Moreover, "they were afraid to ask him" what he meant. They had understood just enough to make them want to avoid that painful subject; and they were afraid to understand more.

Therefore, they left Jesus alone with his disturbing thoughts. They slowed their steps and allowed him to walk ahead of them. And then, when they were alone, they began arguing about their favorite subject: which of the disciples would be the greatest in the Kingdom of Heaven.

Jesus had no need of supernatural power to know what they were discussing. No doubt, the debate became heated. Voices were raised and hard words were exchanged.

When they had reached Capernaum, Jesus asked the disciples, "What were you arguing about on the road?" And, like schoolchildren caught in some prank, the disciples dared not answer him. So, Jesus sat down, called the Twelve to him, and promulgated the Golden Rule of the Kingdom: "If anyone wants to be first, he must make himself last of all and servant of all."

We are like the Apostles. We are "turned off" by counsels of humility. We are repelled by the prospect of humiliation. What society today has as many honorific titles as the Church? Where else can we see so much pomp and pageantry? What other government attaches such importance to protocol and etiquette?

We are no more capable of admitting a God without glory than we are of admitting a leader without prestige. Yet, Jesus abolished man's natural religion by revealing a God who wants to serve rather than be served; a God who does not require us to prostrate ourselves before him but who insists on donning an apron to wash our feet and to wait on our tables. In so doing, Jesus upset our established ideas not only about man's relationship to God, but also about the relationship between leaders and subordinates. And therein lies the originality of Christianity: a God who is meek and humble of heart and who abdicates all his rights in order to serve man.

Man, in his misery, has invented a God cast in the image of his own desires, a God who will compensate for man's own weaknesses. Because man is poor, God must be rich. Because man is weak, God must be omnipotent. Because man suffers, God must be invulnerable and impassive. And because man is dependent, God must be solitary, autonomous, self-sufficient. This God is capable only of compensating for man's insufficiencies and divinizing his ambitions. To imitate such a God, man must strive to become rich, powerful, feared, dominant, invulnerable, and autocratic. And then he will find that he has imitated not God, but the devil.

Jesus demolished the idea of a God who reigns as an almighty sovereign over prostrate humanity. At the same time, he desacralized power, authority, and domination over others. "Among pagans," Jesus warned the Apostles, "it is the kings who lord it over them, and those who have authority over them are given the title Benefactor. This must not happen with you" (Luke 22:25–26).

The Christian knows that if he wishes to be like God, it is not necessary for him to be rich or clever or strong or respected or majestic. All he has to do is to love a bit more and to serve more. Each of us can become God immediately. We can do it in our present walk of life, at our present social and economic level, without even moving from where we are. We can do it simply by becoming the "last of all and servant of all."

It is true that God is almighty. But his might is the strength of love rather than that of power or authority. God is not God because he is the first one served, but because he is the first to serve others.

It is also true that God is transcendent. But his transcendence does not signify distance and domination. It indicates love, service, immanence. It means that no one serves as God serves. No one can give of himself as God gives of himself. No one can love as God loves.

The Apostles found it no easier to understand this than we do. Matthew tells us that, when Jesus made it clear to his disciples that he must suffer and be put to death, "Peter started to remonstrate with him. 'Heaven preserve you, Lord,' he said, 'this must not happen to you'" (16:22). And, even near the end, Peter did not understand: "'Never!'" said Peter. "'You shall never wash my feet'" (John 13:8). Or else they, like we, "did not understand what he said and they were afraid to ask him."

It is our ambition as humans to become "princes of this world." We want to be political or revolutionary leaders, masters of the atom, conquerors of space, explorers and exploiters of matter, of life, of man's conscious, and unconscious mind.

Yet, what is Jesus in comparison to all those who exercise such sovereignty and wield such power? He is a liberation, a mystery of humility which exorcises our passion to conquer and to dominate. He has revealed a grandeur that is not the grandeur of the world, and we stand in amazement before the nobility of the man who would rather wash the feet of the poor or the eyes of the blind than possess "all the kingdoms of the world and their splendor" (Matthew 4:8).

–27–

WHAT WILL BE OUR REWARD?

I tell you solemnly, there is no one who has left house, brothers, sisters, father, children or land for my sake and for the sake of the gospel who will not be repaid a hundred times over . . . not without persecutions—now in this present time and, in the world to come, eternal life. (Mark 10:29–30)

According to the Old Testament, God rewarded the good and punished the wicked here on earth. Life, therefore, had a certain harmony to it since happiness was equated with virtue and punishment with vice. Hardly anyone was interested in a future life which might reward or prolong life on earth. For the ancient Hebrews, there was no impossible contradiction between what man wanted and what man had. Man's ideals could be realized here in this world; and when a man died, he died happy, full of years and surrounded by his offspring.

The ancient Hebrews, in this respect, were not essentially different, at least philosophically, from modern communists. Their interests were encompassed by and rooted in terrestrial life. Certainly, they could not be accused, as Christians are, of trying to escape into another world and of dividing their loyalty between the present life and the life to come.

Obviously, this simplistic concept of life was too much at variance with reality not to awaken doubts among the Hebrews. Too many innocent people suffered, from Abel to Job; too many faithful Jews suffered persecution. Too many cries of agony, distress, and indignation were raised to heaven. And in response to those cries belief in the resurrection was introduced.

And here, in Mark's text, it seems that Jesus himself, the Lamb of God who takes upon himself the sins of the world, the most just and the most long-suffering of men, is confirming the Old Law by promising to return a hundredfold, here and now, in this life, whatever a man gives up for his sake.

However, he added, "not without persecutions."

And he completes the thought by, "eternal life."

Let us not be tempted to believe that Jesus is going back on his previous teaching and confirming the old theories of temporal retribution—theories that the Jews themselves, by Jesus' time, had begun to outgrow by virtue of experience and reflection. On the contrary, Jesus was spiritualizing the traditions of the Hebrews, transforming their temporal Messianism into a universal and spiritual liberation. And at each step of the way it was necessary for him to correct the flatly materialistic mentality of his Apostles.

We should not take literally Jesus' words when he says that a man will be repaid "a hundred times over, houses, brothers, sisters, mothers, children and land." (Matthew and Luke add "wives" to the list of things that will be multiplied a hundredfold. This renders a literal interpretation improbable—and not very enjoyable.) He is obviously referring to goods of another kind, to peace and a joyful conscience, to a happiness compatible with persecution which cannot affect the interior man, and not to the simple satisfactions of material prosperity.

The real problem with Jesus' words, however, lies at the end of the text. What does he mean by "eternal life"? Most people, upon reading those words, believe that Jesus is referring to a future life; and this interpretation has opened up a chasm in Christian existence. The expectation of a future life necessarily devalues the present life. It causes man to be torn between two interests, each of which is weakened because of the energy diverted to the other.

An eternal life is not a future life. It is a present life, a life that transcends ordinary existence but is immanent in the latter—just as God himself is the most transcendent of beings and, at the same time, the being most present to his creatures.

There is no question of choosing between two worlds, but rather of uniting two worlds to such an extent that every moment lived in the temporal world is filled with the spiritual world and that man lives, here and now, a divine life. God does not exist in opposition to the world. God loves the world and permeates it. We are not asked to give up the world, but rather to fill the world with God. That is, to fill it with love.

Such a life will never end. What it will be like in the future —this should concern us less than what it is here and now. The mistake of the eschatologists, as they are called, is to try to imagine the future life and to try to imitate the forms they impute to it. It is as useless for us to try to behave on earth as though we were "glorified bodies" as it would be for an embryo in the womb to try to act as though it were already living its extra-uterine life.

Jesus does not tell us to speculate about the nature of the heavenly Jerusalem. He teaches us to live our daily lives in such a way that we may live forever. He wants our lives to be like his, an inseparable compound of the divine and the human.

All we need to know about the future life is that it will be made up of faith (which is a beginning of sight) and of love. For only love is capable of overcoming death.

Jesus' words, therefore, are intended to send us neither back to the Old Testament nor toward an unknown future. They concern our daily lives as we live them in depth; that is, as we live them after having established relationships between ourselves and other men which are so just and so loving that they may endure forever.

Part Three
SAINT LUKE

–28–

THE BEGINNING, OR THE END?

There will be signs in the sun and moon and stars; on earth nations in agony, bewildered by the clamour of the ocean and its waves; men dying of fear as they await what menaces the world . . . And then they will see the Son of Man coming in a cloud with power and great glory . . . (Luke 21: 25–36)

What a strange text this is, filled with terror, threats, and predictions of catastrophe. And yet, it also contains assurances, hope, and encouragement: "When these things begin to take place," Jesus says, "stand erect, hold your heads high, because your liberation is near at hand."

It is as though Jesus were saying to us: "The world will always be a place of agony and tumult. You will feel that you have been forgotten and that you are lost in the midst of these prodigious upheavals. It will be difficult for you, and often impossible, to see that I am coming, victorious, before the last day. You will see your contemporaries running about, trying to find an escape; but their stars and their signs will not help them then. They will find no salvation, either on earth or in the sea, or even in interstellar space itself.

"Some of them will try to escape through drugs, alcohol, or sexuality. You can already see signs of this around you. Others will try to make use of more prosaic means. They will continue to work frantically in order to amass money, and then work just as frantically to spend it. For the most dangerous drug of the twentieth century is not heroin or LSD; it is work and the pleasure man takes in giving himself over entirely to what the Gospel calls 'the cares of life.'"

There should be a law requiring every businessman to have a sign on the wall of his office, reading: "If I weren't so lazy, I wouldn't work as hard as I do." For work can be an addiction that it is impossible to shake. It can become a routine that dulls our minds and prevents us from thinking; a distraction that relieves us of the burden of being alone with ourselves and asking ourselves questions on things that matter; a means of passing time without having to ask ourselves what we are doing with our time.

Nothing requires more energy and courage than to stop regularly, in the midst of our work, and ask ourselves what we are doing with our lives. This is what Jesus means when he says to us: "Stand erect, hold your heads high." He means that we should rise above our work, no matter how absorbing it may be, so that we may watch and pray in the midst of the enormous throng of robots and automatons that surround us.

The antidote designated in the Gospel for drugs of all kinds is—prayer. Prayer is associated with staying awake, or "watching," because the man who prays must awaken from his mechanical activity and from his carefully cultivated state of unconsciousness. He must discover for the first time the infinite dimensions of his personal destiny and the presence of the One who has been with him for so long but who has remained unrecognized.

Prayer is not a means of escaping from our boredom or our responsibilities. It is not intended to protect us against disaster or to assure divine assistance when we are too weak or too lazy to act for ourselves. It is not an escape into God by means of which we are united to him in forgetfulness of the miseries of existence on earth.

Prayer is simply total realism. It is a panoramic view of reality. Men often see only the unhappiness, the dangers and risks of life, and they cultivate the oblivion that comes from "debauchery and drunkenness and the cares of life" (Luke 21:34). The Christian, on the other hand, while aware of the reality of disorder in the world, is not crushed by what he sees. He also sees reasons for hope and signs of redemption. He knows that the Liberator is alive and that every act of faith and love quickens his coming and brings his Presence closer.

Prayer is an opening of oneself to the whole of reality, and therefore to God's action in history—that action which asks our help so that it may return, just as it asked our help so that it might be born among men.

The man who prays is a man who is sufficiently inspired by the Spirit of God to believe that out of this speck of inert dust, out of this hard stone under his feet, out of the miserable specimens of humanity by which he is surrounded, he can create a world of beauty, harmony, and love.

The man of prayer accepts the whole world and turns toward heaven. He knows what man is, but he never loses hope; for he believes that God so loves the world that he will never abandon it. He believes that God will pursue his plan to transform the world, with the help of all those who are waiting for him and who are working to hasten his Coming.

Though the world may seem to be crumbling around him, the man who prays never gives up his hope or his efforts. He makes very little noise, and he seems terribly alone in the sound and the fury of the mob. But when the world in travail has uttered its final cry and silence comes upon the universe, like the silence of an audience at the solemn moment when the curtain begins to rise, then we will be astonished to see how many men there are still standing erect, their heads high —men worthy of welcoming and celebrating the coming of the Son of Man.

–29–

THE WAYS OF GOD

. . . *A voice cries in the wilderness: Prepare a way for the Lord, make his paths straight . . . winding ways will be straightened and rough roads made smooth.* (Luke 3:1–6)

This passage of the Gospel begins with an imposing list of those in whom the contemporaries of John the Baptist placed their hopes and their fears. It is a litany of illustrious names—the civil, administrative, and religious powers who presided at the appearance of Salvation, who fought it and persecuted it with all their might, and who finally served it without knowing that they were doing so.

Then, in opposition to these distinguished personalities, Luke sketches the image of John the Baptist: a man who belonged to no hierarchy, who had no power or money, and who lived in the desert. As his only weapon, John had the Word that God had spoken to him and to which he had listened so attentively. He had meditated on that Word, and he had lived it so intensely that it was live in him. Alive, and contagious.

Salvation always begins with a word from God, and that word is always addressed to man. What is rare is to find someone who listens to that word and practices it. Most people ignore it. They are preoccupied with more important things: their jobs, their authority, their prestige, their responsibilities, their money. Even a vocation to announce the word of God sometimes serves as a pretext for not taking the time to listen to the word.

For man to be able to live only on the word of God, he must first be reduced to nothingness, to solitude, to the desert, to extreme poverty. "I bless you, Father," Jesus exclaimed, "for hiding these things from the learned and the clever and revealing them to mere children" (Luke 10:21).

This reversal of our human perspective is implicit in the very nature of the "Salvation" announced by the Gospel. All religions have salvation as their purpose. We might even say that all men, in one way or another, try to save themselves; that is, they try to make themselves invulnerable and immortal.

The first means they use it to assert themselves, to intensify the consciousness of their own personal importance, to impose their authority on others, and to gain self-assurance from the reflection of themselves that they see in others. They accumulate fame, riches, prestige, and luxury in order to fill as much place as they can in the short time at their disposal.

But once they have constructed, decorated, and defended their public images, they are left alone with themselves once more; and then they are quickly consumed by boredom. The image they have created closes in on them like a prison. The man who is world-renowned wanted to be loved for himself—like an unknown. The sophisticated urbanite dreams of the simple life in the country. The financier feels that he is a slave to his money. The selfish man complains that no one loves him.

The fundamental need of man is to go outside of himself, to rise above himself and forget himself in a kind of transcendence. Man, unfortunately, can transcend himself in either of two directions: upward, or downward. Modern man, in his need to escape from himself, has recourse to drugs, to pornography, and to violence. He mimes the gestures of love but feels no love. He celebrates, but without joy. He gathers in crowds so as to forget his solitude. He drinks foul water to assuage his thirst for eternity. He attempts to cross the boundaries of himself to regain the innocence of paradise. Our artists disfigure the face of man and make a point of exhibiting his inconsistencies and vices. Our revolutionaries are busily destroying the structures that offer suffering human beings the only shelter they know. Our dissidents reject the habits and prejudices that are part and parcel of the social fabric. And all of these phenomena are manifestations of man's thirst for the infinite, of his intolerance of limitations, of his incurable nostalgia for truth and communication.

Upward transcendence, however, is the only truly liberating transcendence; for only then does man lose himself so as to find himself again in the intensity of being and joy, which is both a gift from God and a discovery of what man possesses deep within himself. True freedom is the ability to say to oneself: It is no longer I who live, but Another who lives in me and makes me more alive than I've ever been. I know now that faith and hope have always been within me, inherent and vital to me, and that I've always struggled against them. Now, I've found within me, in abundance, that which I've always looked for outside of myself. I've opened myself to Another; and that Other has given me back to myself.

With John the Baptist, I want only one thing: "He must grow greater, I must grow smaller" (John 3:30).

The desert, where John was revealed these truths, is symbolic of the poverty, detachment, and self-effacement that is the essential condition for finding true wealth. The sin for which we must repent is not one of those of which we usually accuse ourselves. The only true sin is to be filled with ourselves; to be so content with ourselves that we are unable to open ourselves to God.

Luke's text on John the Baptist is a call to us to repent for this sin. It is an appeal for our conversion and for our discovery of that which the Prophets foretold and proclaimed, but which, in Jesus, is made so alive and immediate that the blind see, the deaf hear, those who could not walk leap to their feet and run to meet him—while good and respectable men like ourselves do not even notice that he has come.

–30–

ON SHARING

What must we do? . . . (Luke 3:10–18)

The whole world loves a hermit. If anyone wants to attract a mob of followers, the first thing he should do is withdraw into a desert. The Stylites, we may be sure, climbed their columns merely to get away from the crowds who had followed them into the desert. And the farther John the Baptist withdrew into the desert, the more he multiplied his austerities, the greater the number of people of all kinds who sought him out.

The modern world is not very different from the ancient world in that respect. Like sheep without a shepherd, we flock to anyone who claims to be "original" or who proclaims himself a revolutionary. Even a simple deformity of mind or body is enough to awaken our interest. And a hint of exoticism is guaranteed to make disciples of those whose ears, as Saint Paul says, itch.

In the case of John the Baptist, the curious and fickle crowds for once stood before a true Master. And, like a Master, John spoke a decisive word which brought each one of his listeners face to face with his own individual truth. John had been asked a question: "What must we do?" What the people wanted was a formula of prayer, or recipe for piety, an ascetic counsel, an encouragement to give alms, or perhaps absolution for their sins. What they got was an answer terrible in its simplicity: "If anyone has two tunics," John said, "he must share with the man who has none, and the one with something to eat must do the same" (Luke 3:11).

All at once, the people realized that John was not playing games. Their curiosity suddenly disappeared. Every man among them had suddenly been stripped of his simulated good will, of his religious sentimentality. Every one of them was forced to look into himself and to take account of what it would cost him to be converted. John had destroyed their illusions concerning the barrier that existed between God and themselves.

All the theological disputations and philosophical debates, all the social and political controversies—all the complex intellectual bric-a-brac that we use to soothe and protect ourselves—all this had suddenly been reduced to a simple, hard question: Can we bring ourselves to share what we have?

Such is the extraordinary effect of God's word. It strips us bare, exposes our hearts as they truly are, leaves us naked before the Father.

We may be sure that those who heard John did not follow up their original question. They had already heard enough to have material for thought, and for agony, for a long time to come. For if there is one sign that we have heard God's word, it is that it hurts; that it reveals what we would prefer not to know; that it touches us in our most sensitive spot. "The word of God is something alive and active: it cuts like any double-edged sword but more finely: it can slip through the place where the soul is divided from the spirit, or joints from the marrow; it can judge the secret emotions and thoughts" (Hebrews 4:12).

The message of John the Baptist is strangely relevant to our own times. It sounds as new and as revolutionary now as it did two thousand years ago. The fundamental problem today is the same as it was then: man is searching for the cause of his anguish in society, in the Church, in the economy, in poverty, and in abundance. And he always finds the remedy in reform—the reform of others.

The true answer, however, is that which John gave to his listeners. We must learn that the evil is in us. The root of all the injustice we see is in our own hearts, and the structures we condemn are nothing more than the reflection of what is in our hearts. When we have brought about the justified destruction of those structures, what will we replace them with? Will our new structures be nothing better than faithful reproductions of our passions, of our lust of possession and domination?

If radical surgery is necessary, then it is we who must first feel the scalpel. Everyone today demands to be allowed to "be themselves," to be free "to do their own thing." This would be a revolution indeed; but before that revolution can be achieved, we must learn self-criticism and self-reform. A man who is alienated from himself has nothing to give except alienation. We must begin, therefore, by establishing real relationships with those around us.

Since man is a network of relationships, he may be judged by the links that bind him to others. If his associates are his slaves, then he himself is a slave. If he is an oppressor, then he is oppressed by his oppression; or possessed by his wealth; or devoured by his greed.

The whole Gospel rests on this maxim of John's: Do you want to be at peace with God? Then be at peace with your neighbor. You are no closer to God than you are to your associates. Your relationships with your fellow men are indicative of your relationship with God. You will be judged, not on the basis of your religious observances, but on that of your social relations. The only proof of your participation with God is your sharing with the poor. This is the meaning of the Incarnation!

If we are to undergo such a revolution, if we are going to destroy everything that encumbers us and limits us, it is not enough for us merely to be willing to do so. It is not enough for us to have a human leader who is too often a projection of ourselves. We must undergo a new birth, a new baptism. There must be another Visitation. We must transform our minds and our hearts. In other words, there must be a new Pentecost.

Only the Spirit of God can renew a man in his innermost being. Only the Spirit can make man accept as natural and necessary that which, left to himself, man regards as horrible and unthinkable. John the Baptist knew it. He readied his audience for the coming of another. He prepared the road for the one who was to come after him. He created the hunger and the thirst that the other was to satisfy. For the Good News was not only a message of light and love, but also the announcement of the coming of the one who would create light and love.

–31–

ON LOVING OUR ENEMIES

Love your enemies, do good to those who hate you, bless those who curse you, pray for those who treat you badly. . . . (Luke 6:27–38)

There were times when Jesus was frightening. Frightening in his logic, frightening in his relentlessness. He went beyond what was said of him; beyond the half-measures at which the Law had quite reasonably stopped. Jesus allowed nothing to stop him. He knows only one law: love. And, from that law, he draws consequences with logic, which must either electrify or repel his followers.

What is our reaction? Are we galvanized, or are we revolted? We should hope that we are one or the other, for then we may be sure that we have at least understood what Jesus had to say. The worst thing that could happen is for us to listen so distractedly that we are unmoved by what we hear.

It is a terrible thing to hear the Word of God and then to reject it. But how much worse it is to accept it and proclaim it liturgically—without even having noted what was said.

Those who do not believe in Jesus are not necessarily lost. They still have a chance. The future is open to them. They may yet be converted. But those who only believe that they believe are irreversibly condemned for they are incapable of imagining that they can and must change.

Jesus' instructions are to love our enemies, to do good to those who hate us. "To the man who slaps you on one cheek," he says, "present the other cheek too; to the man who takes your cloak from you, do not refuse your tunic . . . and do not ask for your property back from the man who robs you." These strong paradoxes are words of salvation for us only when they begin to hurt us. How can we love our enemies when it is only with difficulty that we bring ourselves to love our friends? How can we return good for evil when we can scarcely return good for good? And to pray for those who treat us badly—well, at least that will make us pray occasionally, whereas now we hardly ever pray at all.

So far as turning the other cheek is concerned, we tell ourselves, or letting someone rob us with impunity, these are obviously foolish exaggerations. No one in his right mind would take these injunctions literally.

These things hurt. They hurt because Jesus, in telling us what we must do, has touched us in our most sensitive spot. But we must remember that Jesus also gives us the strength to bear the pain that he inflicts and to do what he says we must do. Certainly, these counsels of perfection are unbearable—so long as they are not preceded by something else; so long as the presence of Jesus and the gift of the Kingdom of God are not already there to balance, justify, and inspire us to do these terrible things.

Jesus said: "How happy are you who are poor" (Luke 6: 20). He did not mean that we should be happy *because* we are poor or sick or insecure. That would be foolish. He meant that we should be happy because he is with us always; because the Kingdom of God is open to us; because he gives us such joy that we are able to bear anything and to regard everything else as unimportant.

"How happy you are," Jesus says—happy, not because things are not going right for us, but because we are no longer orphans and vagabonds. We have become children of God. We have entered the Kingdom to which there is no end. We are the pampered sons of the Father.

Since that is so, we must begin acting like members of the family that we have joined. We must adopt the manners and attitudes of the household. We must give of what we have received so liberally. Since we have been forgiven for all our crimes, we must pardon our enemies for the small harm they have done us. Since we have found the "pearl beyond price," we should sell everything else that we have. Since we have discovered the hidden treasure, we should go joyfully and sell the rest of our possessions. Since we are no longer poor, there is no reason for us to economize. We no longer have to defend ourselves against others so as to keep the little that we have. Now that we are rich beyond our wildest dreams, we should be filled with contagious generosity. We should imitate the divine prodigality. After all, we are now sons of that Father who loves publicans and sinners and takes more joy in one sinner who repents than in a hundred just men who have no need of his forgiveness.

If we cannot enter into the folly of the Gospel, it is because we have not understood and lived the Good News. We can understand these impossible precepts, these terrible commandments, these unbearable demands only once we have lived the wonder of the gift and the forgiveness of God. For these instructions are not addressed to strangers, like a code of laws that we must observe if we want to enter the Kingdom. They are addressed to those who already live within God's family—to those who have already experienced the fact that the Kingdom is given to them as a free gift without any merit or expectation on their part.

If we are repelled by Jesus' words, it is because we are still prisoners of the old religion and the old Law, which enjoined us to do unpleasant and painful things for an absent God. The new Revelation, however, consists in joyous wonder at the incredible things that God does for *us*. We will never be able to finish learning what these things are and permeating ourselves with them. God has taken the initiative. He has canceled out the distance between him and ourselves. He has lavished food upon those who were hungry, and he has invited sinners to share his table.

Once we realize this we will understand that the yoke of Christ is sweet, and his burden light. We will be able to do for others what God has done for us and in us. For the only proof we have that we are truly loved is that we ourselves love. And the only proof we have that we are truly forgiven, that the gift and forgiveness of God lives in us, is that we too are able to forgive.

–32–

ON TEMPTATION

Filled with the Holy Spirit, Jesus left the Jordan and was led by the Spirit through the wilderness, being tempted there by the devil for forty days. . . . (Luke 4:1–13)

How strange this text seems to us. How striking this dialogue, this Scriptural debate between Jesus and the devil. How fantastic it seems—and how far removed from our own lives.

Actually, nothing could be closer to our lives. The narrative of Jesus' temptation in the wilderness is a synopsis of human history and of the history of each of us individually. For the demon begins by saying to Jesus, "If you are the Son of God . . ." The matter at issue here concerns us all: Who is God? How does God (or his Son) prove that he is God? How can we become like God?

Must we become richer and richer, or must we become poorer and poorer through sharing all that we have?

Must we become increasingly independent, or increasingly dependent on those whom we love?

Must we make ourselves more and more invulnerable, or more and more sensitive, attached, accessible?

Must we become more and more aloof, or more and more participants?

Must we be served first, or must we become the first servant? Must we dominate others or set them free? Must we save ourselves, or save others? Must we become the lamb of God who is bled, killed, and eaten, or the wolf who attacks, kills, and devours?

The devil has already made his choice. He loves no one and has no wish to be loved himself. He exists in the terrible tranquility of total solitude. He is independent. And whatever he possesses, that he keeps.

Adam also chose. He took possession of what did not belong to him. He declared his independence. He rebelled and separated himself from God and from his fellow men. (He blamed Eve for his sin. If he had defended her instead, if he had acknowledged his own guilt, he would not have been driven from Paradise—because he would have continued to love!)

Israel, too, chose. In the desert, it chose the calf of god, a "profitable" god, a good investment.

When it was Jesus' turn to choose, Satan offered "success" through strength and prestige. Instead, Jesus chose love, service, and the cross. He is not indifferent to our material problems; but rather than make God responsible for solving them by turning a stone into bread, as the devil asked, Jesus chose to soften our stony hearts by teaching us to share whatever bread we have.

Now that it is our turn, what will our choice be? Who will be our God? How will we be like him? How will we tempt him? By what signs are we willing to recognize him?

Are we like Satan, Adam, and Israel? Will we insist on a display of power? Do we demand miracles—wonders from which we can make a profit? A cure? Success? A promotion? An advantageous marriage? A stroke of luck?

We must be careful of the kind of God we choose. We must remember that we ourselves become the God that we create.

Satan is independent, solitary, rich, strong. We have only to read the Gospels to see what power he gives to his followers. He is the Prince of this world. The kingdoms of the earth are his for the nations rely on force to achieve their aims, and they consult only their own interests. And this idolatry makes them Satan's own.

How weak Jesus seems in comparison to the devil. And how little we are tempted to become like him: trusting, humble, loving, faithful to our Father and our brothers. How little we are tempted to learn how to love, serve, and suffer as he did. Adam desired power without love; but Jesus, on the cross, chose to be love without power.

"Tell this stone to turn into a loaf," the devil told Jesus. How much easier it is to turn stones into bread than to share what we have, as God tells us to do.

Even when Jesus multiplied the loaves and fishes, it was necessary that a child, trusting and naïve, risk the few pieces of bread that he had so that everyone could be given something to eat.

Will it be we Christians who risk what we have so that the great famine of our time can be relieved?

–33–

THE JUST AND THE SINNERS

. . . *The pharisees and the scribes complained. "This man," they said, "welcomes sinners and eats with them."* (Luke 15:2)

I was once preaching to a small gathering in an old cathedral. In the first few rows of pews, there were some nuns and a few laymen. The rest of the congregation was scattered about the church, with many of them standing in the rear—so as to avoid compromising themselves, I suppose.

After reading the Gospel text from Luke's fifteenth chapter, I explained that God's Word is still alive, still pertinent, still revelatory. Then I explained: "The publicans and the sinners and prostitutes were always standing in the first rows of the crowd to hear him . . ."

Immediately, there was a mild sensation in the church. The people in the first pews blushed and stared at the floor. Those standing in the back shuffled their feet and smiled in self-congratulation.

I looked at those in the rear of the church. "The Scribes and the Pharisees," I went on, "complained about Jesus, saying, 'This man welcomes sinners and eats with them.'"

It was the standees' turn to stare at the floor.

I was astonished to discover that a reading of the Gospel

before a congregation of Christians had the effect of making everybody unhappy!

We know perfectly well that we are sinners; but we take satisfaction only in thinking that we are counted among the just. If we are told that the just are not invited to the Wedding of the Lamb, we take it as a personal affront. But when the privileges of the sinner are proclaimed, which of us take pleasure in hearing them? Before receiving the Eucharist, we all tell God that we are not worthy of receiving him. But what would happen if the priest took us at our word and refused to give us communion? One can only imagine the scene that would ensue. "He took advantage of my humility to humiliate me!" we would complain. What an unusual kind of humility it must be that we are talking about . . .

The sterility of our religious life may perhaps be explained by this basic misunderstanding. Christianity is made for sinners, and we have turned it into the religion of the just. We say that we are Christians because we are virtuous, honest, irreproachable. In our hearts, we think that we are better than non-Christians. And yet, we are really Christians only because—only *if*—we admit that we are sinners.

The faith is full of terrible paradoxes. Many people think they are unworthy of being called Christians because they are so weak and sinful. But an even greater number of people will never be Christians precisely because they regard themselves as just, honest, and superior to other people. Some people think that because they are sinners it would be hypocritical of them to practice their religion. But many more cut themselves off from Christianity because they do not recognize that they are sinners. Having excluded all these people from Christianity, we may well ask if there is anyone left.

Many, indeed. For the Redemption was not undertaken for the sake of the just, but so that those who were lost might be found and saved. Those who are healthy have no need of a doctor. Only the sick require medical attention.

For the first Christians, the Gospel was Good News: God had granted free pardon for sins! Everyone rejoiced. Conversions were published and celebrated everywhere. The announcement of pardon, and the recital of sins, quite naturally became the material of the preface of the Eucharistic banquet. In the New Testament, confessions and conversions were the occasion for joyous celebrations. Matthew invited publicans and sinners. Zachaeus gave a supper for Jesus, and Mary Magdalene, Lazarus, and Martha received him at their table.

Our customs are different today. A man no longer takes his confessor home with him for supper. He no longer tells his wife: "That confession was really something! It was a wonderful experience! I feel absolutely great! Let's have a drink to celebrate!"

For us modern Christians, the Gospel is bad news. We are shocked to learn that we are sinners in need of forgiveness. "Forgiven?" we ask indignantly. "Forgiven for what?" Sometimes, out of good will or docility, we pretend to admit that, in our own small way, we may be sinners. Then we pretend to be happy because we are forgiven. And all the religion we have lies there and is lost between those two moments of hypocrisy.

What a glorious change it would be if, during Sunday mass, we sincerely acknowledged that we are sinners and we celebrated the wonders that God has worked in his lowly servants. Then we would truly be able to offer thanks. We would compete in praising the only Being who is good. What a relief that would be from the pervasive hypocrisy that is smothering us! How wonderful it would be if every Christian rose and recounted how he came to church and how he almost did not come; who brought him and how he tried to get out of attending mass; how he has often sinned and how, each time, Jesus has brought him back by patient invitation, gentle solicitation, and by his messengers and prophets. We would then be like the first Christians, gathered together to edify one another by bearing witness to the mercy of God.

The only truly Christian joy is the knowledge that we have been forgiven. The only justifiable astonishment is that which accompanies the discovery that God is so much better than we are.

We will go to heaven, be saved, and be eternally happy, not because we are content with ourselves, but because we are content with God, enthusiastic about our Savior, dazzled by his forgiveness. Then we will spend eternity telling about our repentance rather than boasting about our virtues and our apostolic exploits. Peter, in heaven, tells everyone how he betrayed and abandoned his Master; how he stubbornly denied him three times; and how a single glance from Jesus brought him back and regenerated him. "And do you know what he gave me for a penance?" Peter asks. "You'll never guess. He made me head of the Church!"

Then, each saint rises in turn to celebrate the Lord by describing the pardon that he himself has received; for that is the most beautiful eulogy that can be spoken.

We too will be tempted to speak, to announce that we too have something to say, something to contribute to this celebration: our account of the sins that have been forgiven. Our hymn of praise and thanksgiving will consist in that account. That is, if we can bear even then to confess our sins in such a public ceremony . . .

–34–

THE GOODNESS OF THE FATHER

. . . It is only right we should celebrate and rejoice, because your brother here was dead and has come to life; he was lost and is found. (Luke 15:11–32)

Only God knows how to forgive sins.

Certainly, it is also true to say, "Only God can forgive sins"; but that way of phrasing it seems to imply some sort of magisterial power or judicial junction which is unbecoming to God.

It is better to say that only God knows *how* to forgive sins. To know how to forgive is much more important than having the power to forgive. It is more difficult to persuade a sinner to accept pardon than it is to offer pardon when we have been offended. The position of the one who forgives is elevated, honorable, superior; but that of the one who is pardoned is painful and humiliating—so much so that to forgive is often equivalent to creating a permanent resentment.

There are pardons so lofty, so exasperating, that the one who is pardoned will never pardon the pardoner. One who forgives must exercise infinite tact and contagious humility. He must be overflowing with affection so as not to wound the one he is forgiving. He should say, in effect: "Please forgive me for forgiving you. I'm doing it because I want to be at peace with myself. Please do me the favor of accepting my forgiveness—and forgive me for offering it so clumsily. Let's forget all about it and celebrate because we are together again."

Does this seem exaggerated? Paradoxical? Impractical?

But that is exactly God's way of forgiving! The parable of the lost or "prodigal" son and the dutiful son reveals that God excuses and humiliates himself in order to have his forgiveness accepted.

The distorted religious education we have received often makes us think of ourselves as repentant sinners begging a stern God for forgiveness. The truth is that God can hardly wait to forgive us. God *begs* us to accept his pardon. And we resist, refuse, and flee.

Even so, God wants so strongly to reinstate us in his friendship that his desire to forgive finally awakens in us a wish to be forgiven and a desire to provide God with the incomparable joy of a sinner who repents.

The case of the prodigal son in the parable is relatively simple. This son preferred the tangible realities of money and women to the perhaps monotonous satisfactions of family life. It may have been that the father was weak in giving in to his son's demands. But if he had tried to keep his son at home by force, or if he had allowed him to leave home penniless and angry, would he ever have seen him again?

Nonetheless, when the son finally returns to his father's house, it is not out of filial affection or because he truly repents of what he has done. It is because he has nowhere else to go. He has no money left. The most he hopes for is to be allowed to eat with his father's servants.

Because he himself has no love, he cannot imagine or admit that his father still loves him. He does not even think of himself as a son any longer. His emotions are dead. He is truly a lost son.

Jesus' parable tells us what a Father must do to resurrect a son who was dead. It shows us how to forgive, how to go about getting someone to accept our forgiveness so that the affection with which we forgive wins the heart of the one who is forgiven. The son in the parable becomes a son again because he is won over by the tenderness of the father.

The father is certainly more patient than the son is repentant. The father "ran to the boy, clasped him in his arms and kissed him tenderly." He interrupted the boy's well-rehearsed confession to give him new clothing and shoes and even a ring.

We may well ask ourselves if we have ever exercised forgiveness in this way.

Yet, all these things were necessary if the son, hardened by his experiences, was to be won over. He compares his own hardness of heart to his father's generosity (the father is the one who is the real "prodigal" in this parable) and allows himself to respond to his father's affection.

It is only then that he is home for good; that he has become a son once more, open, loving, and trusting. It is only then that the father is able to say that his son, who was dead, had come to life.

This is a kind of resurrection that few of us are capable of working.

The case of the dutiful son in the parable is more difficult. That son, unfortunately, is a just man. But he is also sour, jealous, easily moved to anger—and a complainer. He thinks that his brother is better off than he. Secretly, he envies his brother the sins that he himself has not had the courage to commit. What he really regrets is that he didn't do the same thing that his brother did.

The dutiful son's character, as depicted by Luke, awakens very little sympathy in us. We are immediately suspicious even of his virtues, and we are certain that he is hardhearted. Our advice to his father would be to treat him harshly, to give him a lecture on how corrupt his conscience is and how the wine of his virtue has turned to vinegar.

But God is not like us. Only God knows how to forgive sins, even the irritating sins of those who do not admit that they are sinners. God is the one who turns the other cheek, and who offers his tunic to the robber who has stolen his cloak.

How does the father deal with his dutiful son? "His father came out to plead with him." We would expect the father to be angry, to punish the boy. But then, the son would never have repented. His father's anger would have reinforced his own. He would have felt bitterness and undying resentment. He would have been certain that his father did not understand him, that he had been treated outrageously. And he would never have forgiven either his brother or his father.

But the father knew how to handle his son. He spoke to him with great tenderness and affection: "My son, you are with me always, and all I have is yours." He even excuses himself: "It was only right that we should celebrate," he pleads, as though to say, "What else could I do?"

We can only believe that, before his father's unexpected humility and tenderness, the dutiful son felt his anger ebb away. In amazement, he repeated to himself those marvelous words: "You are with me always. All I have is yours." And, comparing the boundless generosity of the Father with his own petty selfishness, he understood that he had sinned and he became a son once more.

The Father resurrected both his sons through love and forgiveness. There is a forgiveness that kills, and a forgiveness that gives life. Only the Father knows that a sinner has need of much more than simple forgiveness. He needs to be loved and to be given life. He needs to be taught to forgive himself for having sinned and to forgive us for having forgiven him. He needs to rebuild everything in himself that sin has destroyed.

And that is a work that only God knows how to do.

–35–

MARTHA AND MARY

. . . It is Mary who has chosen the better part; it is not to be taken from her. (Luke 10:38–42)

The Gospel account of Martha and Mary is one that often offends busy wives and mothers—to say nothing of busy single people. We all know many Marys who are mysteriously absent when there are meals to be cooked or tables to be set or dishes to be washed. It is hard to say whether or not these Marys have really "chosen the better part." All that we know for certain is that there are uncounted Marthas, overwhelmed by work and worry, who would give anything for a few moments of rest and meditation.

The fact is that the opposition between Martha and Mary was not created by the Gospel. It has resulted from a distorted interpretation of Luke's account. Mary was not a lazy woman or an inactive one. One can be both contemplative and active. The founders of the great religious orders found in prayer the enormous energy and inspiration required for their voyages, their struggles, and their apostolic work. Saint John tells us (11:29; 31) that when Jesus asked for Mary, she "got up quickly and went to him." And we know that, on the day after the Resurrection, she was the first to go to

Jesus' tomb—before dawn, "while it was still dark." Then she ran to tell Peter and John what she had seen.

Mary was an active woman. But when Jesus wanted to talk to her, what could possibly have been more important than to listen to him?

We know that listening to the Lord is not very popular. People do not stand in line to listen to sermons or to attend retreats. And we know, too, that listening to God's Word is rarely relaxing or enjoyable. "The Word of God is something alive and active: it cuts like any double-edged sword, but more finely: it can slip through the place where the soul is divided from the spirit, or joints from the marrow; it can judge the secret emotions and thoughts" (Hebrews 4:12). The Word of God reveals, strips: "You are pruned already, by means of the word that I have spoken to you" (John 15:3). There can be nothing requiring more activity, and nothing more painful, than to allow the Spirit to work in us so that it may raise us from the dead.

And that was the pain which Martha was not able to bear.

Martha was not really an activist. She was one of those people who must always be doing something. She could not bring herself to sit quietly while Jesus spoke, so that his words could do their work of revelation, transformation, and renewal within her. Probably, she thought he talked too much, and she found his words tiresome. In her heart, she felt that he was trying to lead her where she was unwilling to go; that he was trying to transform her into a new woman—a deep, thoughtful, and calm person, which she had no intention of allowing herself to become.

So, unable to remain sitting quietly, she rose and busied herself in the kitchen, stirring her food, hanging her kettles, and bustling about. Finally, unable to bear the thought that her sister, Mary, was doing what she had been unable to do —Mary was eagerly drinking in the words that Martha had been unable to understand—Martha brusquely interrupted Jesus and asked him to reprimand Mary.

Jesus' answer was extraordinarily patient and kind: "Martha, Martha, you worry and fret about so many things, and yet few are needed, indeed only one. It is Mary who has chosen the better part; it is not to be taken from her." One might have expected Jesus to be less gentle with Martha. He could have "put her in her place." He could have told her frankly what was really troubling her. Instead, he contented himself with defending Mary's choice and with encouraging that choice.

Martha's mistake was not that she was working, but that she was unwilling to allow God's word to work within her. It was not that she was too active, but only that she was too busy. She was not wrong in serving Jesus and Mary, but only in not leaving them in peace.

Jesus certainly was no advocate of laziness and sloth. "Happy that servant when his master's arrival finds him at this employment," he says (Luke 12:43). And, at the same time, Jesus reproaches those who have not made good use of the talents they have received. But he knows that nervous activity, agitation, impatience, and fear are the worst enemies of good work.

It happened once that Jesus found Mary in a state of agitation and worry because she thought him dead and, being unable to find him, was searching everywhere. She was so upset that when Jesus finally appeared to her she did not even recognize him. On that occasion, Jesus reprimanded her for her lack of joy, faith, and peace. He told her to calm herself, to take hold of herself. Then, as soon as she was in control of herself again, as soon as she had recognized Jesus, he sent her back to tell the others. He made her, as it were, an apostle to the Apostles.

The real distinction of Mary, the better part she chose which was not to be taken from her, did not consist in happiness as that quality is commonly understood. When a woman called out to Jesus: "Happy the womb that bore you and the breasts you sucked," Jesus replied: "Still happier those who hear the word of God and keep it!" (Luke 11:27–28).

–36–

ON PRAYER

Lord, teach us to pray . . . (Luke 11:1–13)

Jesus prayed often. There were many times when he wanted nothing more than to be alone, away from the fickle crowds and from his turbulent and quarrelsome apostles. Occasionally, he managed to slip away to a solitary place, to a mountain or a desert. And, when evening came, he was there, alone with his Father.

There was nothing he had to ask of the Father. Neither bread, nor forgiveness, nor protection, nor gifts. But, in the presence of the Father, Jesus became himself once more. He regained his interior tranquility. He was able to listen in the depths of his soul. The awareness of his divine sonship filled him with strength and gladness. He recognized once more that he was the well-loved son of the Father, and that the Father had covered him with gifts. He felt that he was once more filled with the divine patience and boundless mercy of the Father, and with his vital, creative love. His prayer was one of trust and affection: "Father, I thank you for hearing my prayer. I knew indeed that you always hear me" (John 11:41–42).

Then, when Jesus returned, refreshed and renewed, to the

Apostles, they asked one another: "Where has he been? What could have happened to him? What could have changed him so much?" Someone answered: "He went off alone to pray." And the others said: "Ah, if only we could learn to pray like that!"

Finally, someone said to Jesus, "Lord, teach us to pray."

Jesus therefore taught them a prayer that was similar to his own prayer ("Father, may your name be held holy, your kingdom come . . .") but which he adapted to their particular needs: "give us each day our daily bread, and forgive us our sins, for we ourselves forgive each one who is in debt to us. And do not put us to the test" (Luke 11:2–4).

The prayer which he gave them was not one to be recited, but to be meditated. After all, Jesus himself required an entire night to pray a single sentence to the Father: "Let your will be done, not mine" (Luke 22:43). It was a prayer intended to germinate within the Apostles and to transform them, to lead them toward the prayer of total and happy consent which Jesus himself prayed in his moments of solitary meditation.

Immediately thereafter, in the familiar and informal style that was his very own, Jesus told the Apostles the story of the importunate friend. Only Jesus knew the Father well enough to be able to speak of him so lightheartedly, to be able to compare the Father to a humble housewife who has lost a coin, or to a shepherd who has lost a sheep, or to an impatient and unjust judge; or, in this case, to a tepid, grumbling friend. It is the kind of language that members of a family use among themselves; a language which, when used in the presence of outsiders, has to be translated into terms the latter can understand. Thus, a habit, or a dominant trait can be described satirically. A virtue can be travestied so that it appears to be an amusing weakness; an ability to concentrate can be described as absent-mindedness; and a rare quality of character can be transformed into an innocent idiosyncrasy.

When described in this spirit, God is so good that he sometimes appears weak to those who look at things superficially. He is so affectionate that he cannot say "no" to anyone. He is so devoted to us that we can twist him around our little finger.

Jesus, still speaking a language that we can understand, attacks our skepticism and defiance. He scoffs at our timidity and assures us that there is no limit to the divine generosity. He tells us that our desires are limited only by our fears, our prayers by our weakness, and our achievements by our lack of faith. If we fail, it is not because God has failed us.

The obstacle to having our prayers answered is not the difficulty of getting God to listen to them, but the difficulty of getting ourselves to pray with faith. We must persevere in prayer, not to wear down the Father's resistance to giving, but to wear down our own resistance in taking. But the fact that God always answers our prayers should not awaken our greed or make us more selfish than we already are. The only thing that we can pray for, and the only thing that God can give us, is himself: his Spirit, his Love.

The gifts of God must be handled with care. They are alive, vital, surprising—dangerous to our egotism and our laziness. The gift of God is to enable us to give. The forgiveness of

God is to enable us to forgive. The love of God enables us to love as God loves, even to the passion and the cross.

That is the only true prayer. And perhaps that is why the very thought of prayer frightens us so; for we know that our prayers are always answered.

–37–

THE WOES OF THE RICH

. . . Watch, and be on your guard against avarice of any kind, for a man's life is not made secure by what he owns, even when he has more than he needs. . . . (Luke 12:13–21)

In the parable of the rich man, related in this text of Luke, God declares that a man who places his trust in riches is a fool.

Was God talking about us?

Jesus' words on the accumulation of riches, if we dared repeat them publicly today, would have a very special application. They are aimed straight at the heart of our consumer society, at our profit-oriented economy, at our mania for producing without once stopping to wonder what kind of man and what kind of life it is that we are producing.

Even in Jesus' time it was not easy to be a rich man. Wealth does not bring peace. On the contrary, it awakens the urge to accumulate ever greater wealth. It creates the need to protect what one has. And, finally, it raises the problem of finding ways to spend one's money. The rich man is loaded down with his wealth, like a camel is loaded down with cargo when it tries to pass through a low, narrow gate. The camel, however, is a sensible animal. When it stands before such a gate, it allows its burden to be lifted from its back. But the rich man insists on keeping his load on his back. He grows angry if anyone tries to relieve him of it. In fact, he loudly demands that the load be made even heavier.

What the rich man wants more than anything else is to create a permanent home for himself here on earth, to erect a lasting abode. What he acquires, he acquires forever. What he possesses, he keeps forever. Whereas, if the rich man were truly wise, he would live as he would like to live forever, in the friendship of God and of those with whom he should share what he has.

It should be said, and repeated frequently, that the sin of the rich man is not that he has wealth. Goods are—good. The Redeemer does not contradict the Creator. Everything that exists is good; and everything that exists is here for us to use. Jesus himself promised to reward his followers with goods: "I tell you solemnly, there is no one who has left house, brothers, sisters, father, children or land for my sake and for the sake of the gospel who will not be repaid a hundred times over, houses, brothers, sisters, mothers, children and land—not without persecutions—now in this present time and, in the world to come, eternal life" (Mark 10:29–30). And when Jesus asked his Apostles whether, when he sent them out to preach, they had ever lacked money, or food, or shoes, they replied that they had not.

Jesus, therefore, does not expect us to strip ourselves of all worldly goods. What we must do is to learn to use these goods as they should be used. We should make them serve us. We should use them for the benefit of others. We should use them to make friends for ourselves and collaborators in the utilization of our wealth.

Wealth is a sin only when it is accumulated for its own sake. When we keep it exclusively for our own use, when we become slaves to wealth.

On the other hand, it is a terrible thing to be entirely without goods of any kind. Privation is a condition against which we should protect both ourselves and others, for it too, like wealth, becomes a burden, a torment, and a form of slavery which prevents us from being free and open to God, to our fellow men, and to ourselves.

The man who is poor, not in goods but in his heart, is a happy man. The man who has possessions, but does not become their slave, is a happy man. And the man who is openhanded, rather than empty-handed, is a happy man!

The rich man, by definition, is not a man whose hands are full. A man's hands can be full and, at the same time, open. And the poor man is not a man whose hands are empty, for our hands can be simultaneously empty and closed. In God's eyes, the poor man is the one whose hands are open, regardless of whether they are full or empty. Such a man expects all, gives all, and receives all—a hundredfold. There have been many saints who were great accumulators of wealth and, at the same time, equally great distributors of wealth.

It is not important whether our houses are palaces or shacks. Only one thing matters: Are our doors open? If we can answer, "Yes," then we are poor. But if we barricade ourselves in our houses and build a fortress of our goods, then we are rich. If we build in order to protect what we have, we are rich. And when death comes to eject us from our fortress, we will see ourselves as we truly are: terribly naked and horribly alone. At that moment, we will recognize our folly for what it is. But then it will be too late.

–38–

THE LOST SHEEP

. . . *Rejoice with me* . . . *I have found my sheep that was lost.* . . . (Luke 15:3–7)

Jesus habitually made use of parables because his listeners would not have been able to bear it if he had presented, as a law and as divine revelation, the truths that he insinuated into these stories. They were willing to admit something about a shepherd's feeling for his sheep that it would have shocked them even to think concerning God's feelings for man. And yet, this revolutionary parable of the lost sheep goes to the very heart of the Gospel and enables us to understand why, for some, it is such Good News.

We are transported into a new world, a world of paradoxes in which the first are last and the last are first, where the man who loses is the winner and the man who wants to save his life loses it. We begin to sense something of the originality of the Kingdom and of the joy that reigns there. It is the joy of freedom and generosity, the joy of a mercy greater than any that was ever known—the same mercy that Jesus accuses the Pharisees, in the parables of the prodigal son and the laborers in the vineyard, of neither understanding nor sharing.

God is supremely free. He distributes his gifts where he

will, according to his generous inspirations and creative impulses. His methods defy all calculation. They are infinitely beyond anything that we are able to grasp. Only one thing can limit his liberality: our refusal to accept his gifts. This refusal often exists among the just who, from habit, regard their virtue as their private, inalienable property. They forget that if they are just, they owe their justice to God's munificence. They think of virtue as something that is theirs by right; and they resent anyone else who makes a claim to virtue. They feel that God is really being too weak and indulgent toward sinners. They are like the second or third generation of a *nouveau riche* family who regard with contempt those who, through their own efforts, have just succeeded in attaining the same rank as themselves.

If we were going to stage a production of the Last Judgment, we could place the just outside the gates of Heaven, milling about, impatient to enter. They are sure of their reward, proud of their goodness. Then, suddenly, a rumor spreads through the crowd: "They say he's forgiving all the others, too!" The initial stupefaction of the just gives way to indignation. They complain, grow angry, and begin to mutter among themselves: "A fat lot of good it did us to deprive ourselves of so many things! If only we had known! They should have told us beforehand! We've been made fools of!" Then, they begin to curse God—and are damned on the spot.

Judgment has taken place. God has shown himself in the form that the just should have learned to recognize: as dispensing the forgiveness that they themselves so often received. They should have recognized the mercy that God so often exercised toward them. But they do not; for they have lost the feeling for God, the taste for God. For that reason, they must remain eternally incapable of sharing God's joy in dispensing mercy and forgiveness.

There are even sinners who refuse to accept God's mercy. Some of us are so blinded by our sins that we think we have no need of mercy. We are perfectly content in our misery, and we are surprised that anyone would suggest we might want to change.

There are some who refuse to accept forgiveness because they think they are unworthy of it. These are Pharisees-in-reverse, so to speak. The garden variety of Pharisee thinks he is worthy of being loved because he is virtuous. The sinner-Pharisee admits the same principle: he is loved only if he deserves to be loved. But he applies this principle differently, saying that God cannot love him because he does not deserve God's love. He forbids God to pardon him, explaining that he is only a sinner. "God can't really be interested in someone like me," he seems to say. "I'm too wicked for him."

All of these people, just and sinners alike, refuse to believe in the spontaneous eruption of divine prodigality, in the joy that God experiences in giving and forgiving. God is himself only when he gives, and only when he gives in the most perfect way; that is, by forgiving. That is the reason why there is so much joy in heaven over God's exercise of forgiveness. God never speaks, never reveals himself so clearly as when he forgives; and so, those who love God make a great feast at the appearance of that which lies deepest in the heart of the one they love.

In order to participate in that joy, we must resemble God within ourselves. We must have a natural interior movement that corresponds to that divine exercise. We must have a taste for giving and forgiving. Jesus himself assures us that the Last Judgment will be based upon that same common spirit and common experience. To all those who have given, God will give in return, according to the degree in which they have opened themselves to him by opening themselves to their brothers. All those who have forgiven will be forgiven in turn. The fact that they have exercised forgiveness will be accepted as proof that they have learned to love by virtue of the frequent forgiveness they have received. Those who have refused to judge their brothers will not even be judged. They will enter into heaven without having to pass any tests or trials, because their respect for others, their indulgence, and their love will already have placed them in communication with the God of mercy.

Thus, it is up to us to decide what God's attitude will be toward us. We chose the scale on which we will be weighed. We dictate the sentence that God will impose upon us—so long as we are permeated by the freedom and the generosity of his Spirit.

–39–

ON GRATITUDE

. . . Stand up and go on your way. Your faith has saved you. (Luke 17:11–19)

Jesus regarded it as a duty—and perhaps as a source of some pleasure to him—to take advantage of every opportunity to call the Jews to task for their pride in regarding themselves as God's chosen people and as his favorite sons. He praises the faith of a pagan. He declares that he prefers the charity of a Samaritan to the legalism of the priests and levites. He says that the publicans and prostitutes will be the first to enter the Kingdom of Heaven. And here, in the passage from Luke which describes Jesus' cure of the lepers, Jesus contrasts the behavior of the one Samaritan leper with that of the nine Jews who were also cured of their disease.

Certainly, Jesus was sent only to "the lost sheep of Israel," as he says with a touch of regret; but he announces the opening of the Kingdom to a host of foreigners who will take the place of those who were first invited.

What Jesus admired about the pagans was their freshness of heart, the absence of that pride in being the elect of God which characterized the Jews. And he delighted in their capacity for wonder and in their openness to grace.

In the account of the lepers, ten men were cured. But to only one of them did Jesus say: "Your faith has saved you." No doubt, the other nine must have experienced at least a moment of faith; otherwise, they would not have been cured. But that moment was too brief to effect their salvation. The difference between them and the Samaritan was that the faith of the latter resulted in a feeling of gratitude. Grace not only places us in a state of grace, but also moves us to give thanks. The Christian is not a man who asks for grace or receives grace. He is a man who gives thanks. The Eucharist is the central act of the liturgy; and the great Christian prayer is one of thanksgiving.

All nations pray, and all religions ask for favors. Christianity is different in that it can be described as a religion of thanksgiving. Christian prayer is an act of acknowledgment that one has received infinitely more than he could ever have asked for. It is the recognition that the Father knows better than we what we need. It is the constant taking of inventory of the great things that God has achieved in us, his poor servants. It is the revelation to others of all the gifts that God has given us.

The Samaritan who was cured of leprosy came back to Jesus, "praising God at the top of his voice and threw himself at the feet of Jesus and thanked him." That is how we should pray!

Nietzsche reproached Christians for not *looking* as though they are saved. And he was right, of course. Our joy is not so obvious as to bear witness to the blessings we have received; and our generosity certainly does not attest to the magnitude of God's gifts to us.

The problem is that our prayers are too often nothing more

than a list of complaints. When Christians ask the celebrant of the Eucharistic feast to pray for their intentions, it almost invariably happens that those intentions are a catalogue of catastrophes, fears, and sufferings. Prayer seems to be a time for conjuring up everything that is worst in our lives.

Obviously, even this is better than nothing. It is better than indifference; and it is certainly better than despair. But, unfortunately, that is precisely what the nine other lepers did. And we know that their faith was not sufficient to save them.

We begin to be Christians when we begin expressing our gratitude to God. We bear witness to the grace we have received by celebrating our Liberation. We become sons of God only when we dare say to the Father: "I know that you always hear me. I know that you have already heard me. I know that everything that is yours is mine also."

We must keep in mind that thanksgiving is not only a prayer or a ceremony. To give thanks is, above all, an *act*.

There is considerable misunderstanding on this point. When we see someone who has received the Eucharist remain quietly in his pew, his eyes closed, we can be sure that, if we asked him what he was doing he would reply: "I am making an act of thanksgiving." That is all very well. But the fact is that he is not making an *act* of thanksgiving. What he is doing is allowing himself to be filled with God's grace. He is being passive. An act of thanksgiving should be like that of the grateful Samaritan. It should take place in the middle of the street, outside of the church. And it should not only be expressed in words. It should take the form of a contagious joy. It should not only describe the gifts we have received, but also display those gifts by communicating them to others.

The world will know what we have received only if we share our wealth. People will believe that we have been cured only if the cure is more contagious than the disease. They will believe that our Savior is alive only when they are saved by him, through us.

–40–

ZACCHAEUS

. . . Today salvation has come to this house, because this man too is a son of Abraham; for the Son of Man has come to seek out and save what was lost. (Luke 19:1–10)

In Luke's narrative concerning Zacchaeus, Jesus enters the town of Jericho and, for once, he is given a warm welcome. A crowd gathers around him, and people ask him to visit their houses and stay with them.

But Jesus is pitiless in unmaking illusions. He sees superficial good intentions for what they are, and refuses the invitations of those who act out of self-interest. All the most respectable citizens of the town were there, but Jesus will have none of them. Instead, he spies a man who has climbed a tree to get a better view of the famous prophet—a man too short to see from the ground—and he stops under the tree and looks up. "Zacchaeus," he calls out, "come down! Hurry, because I must stay at your house today!"

There was an instant commotion in the crowd. Zacchaeus was not only a publican, but the chief of the publicans; a man despised by all, greedy, dishonest, a collaborator with the enemy. His fellow citizens would not have touched him with a ten-foot pole, for he was contaminated by the company he kept and by his wealth. Yet, Jesus chose him above everyone else.

Why? Is it to reward Zacchaeus for taking the trouble to climb the tree? There is no reason to believe so. The man had probably acted out of nothing more than curiosity. Perched up in his tree, he certainly wanted to do no more than see Jesus. Certainly, conversation would have been difficult. (If he had wanted to talk to Jesus, he would no doubt have done so in secret.) And it was unlikely that he had any hope of hearing a sermon while hanging from a branch.

Jesus did not intend to reward Zacchaeus for his merits. Indeed, he intended to allow the publican to acquire merit. Zacchaeus thought that he had seen Jesus; but it was Jesus who had seen Zacchaeus. And it was Jesus who called to this public sinner, this pariah, this lonely and despised man. "Zacchaeus," he shouted gaily, and perhaps with a touch of affectionate malice, "Zacchaeus! Come down! Hurry!"

Since Zacchaeus was chief of the publicans, it is likely that he was no longer a young man. We know that he was short, and that he was rich. And we may conclude that climbing trees was not his favorite form of exercise. Actually, climbing up a tree is hard enough; but climbing down is something else again. And here was Jesus, telling him to hurry.

So Zacchaeus took his courage in both hands and scrambled down as fast as he could, overcome with amazement and delight. Jesus knew his name! He had sought him out! He had passed over everyone else and invited himself to his house! He would spend the day there, eating and drinking and talking!

Zacchaeus was shaken to the bottom of his soul. Suddenly, all of his values were turned upside down. He was so overwhelmed by Jesus' generosity, by the divine prodigality, that he felt as though he was being swept away. When the people began to complain that Jesus was going to stay in a sinner's house, "Zacchaeus stood his ground and said to the Lord: 'Look, sir, I am going to give half my property to the poor, and if I have cheated anybody I will pay him back four times the amount.'" Clearly, this was more than Zacchaeus could afford; but he could not keep himself from doing for others what Jesus had just done for him. He wanted the poor and those he had cheated to feel the same surprise and joy that Jesus had made him feel.

Jesus was able to love Zacchaeus because he could love gratuitously, without reason, purely out of the goodness of his heart. For Zacchaeus was a man who was also able to love. Until then, he had always waited for others to love him before he offered his love in return; but now, he suddenly understood that he should not wait, that he should make the first move. And so, he made it.

Everyone thought that Zacchaeus was a miser, whereas he was essentially a generous man. Previously, he had enjoyed amassing wealth. Now, he delighted in giving it away.

Such is the effect wrought by Jesus. He revealed the goodness hidden within every man. He makes people be born to a new life. He resurrects the dead—and especially those who are the deadest of all; i.e., those who mistakenly believe that they are alive. Jesus knows that no one is what he would like to be, and that we must be given an abundance of love before we become capable of loving. Jesus loves all those whom no one else wants to love, whom no one else thinks worthy of love or capable of love. And, because of that extraordinary generosity, he evokes in them a torrent of love, generosity, and joy that no one would have thought possible.

Jesus ignored the complaints of those standing around him and Zacchaeus. After all, from which of those respectable citizens could he have gotten the kind of response he had just awakened in Zacchaeus? And, we might add, from which of us?

What John the Baptist had said was true: "I tell you, God can raise children for Abraham from these stones!" (Luke 3:8). For Jesus made a son of Abraham out of the hard, greedy man who had been Zacchaeus. And then he made a great show of him before all the people, like the Father of the prodigal son who exclaimed to his servants: "This son of mine was dead and has come back to life; he was lost and is found!" (Luke 15:24).

DATE DUE

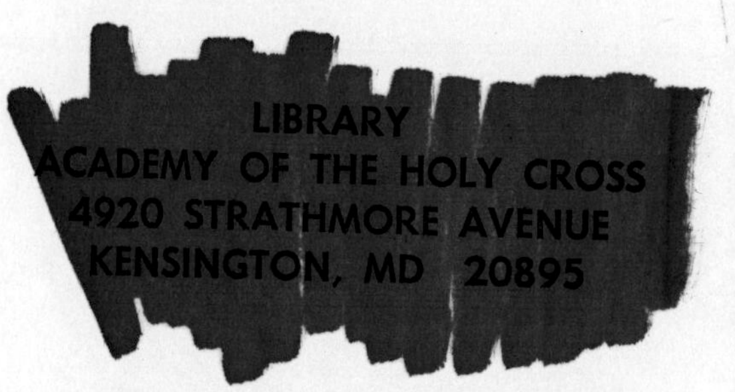
LIBRARY
ACADEMY OF THE HOLY CROSS
4920 STRATHMORE AVENUE
KENSINGTON, MD 20895